Oil and America's Securi

Brookings Dialogues on Public Policy

The presentations and discussions at Brookings conferences and seminars often deserve wide circulation as contributions to public understanding of issues of national importance. The Brookings Dialogues on Public Policy series is intended to make such statements and commentary available to a broad and general audience, usually in summary form. The series supplements the Institution's research publications by reflecting the contrasting, often lively, and sometimes conflicting views of elected and appointed government officials, other leaders in public and private life, and scholars. In keeping with their origin and purpose, the Dialogues are not subjected to the formal review procedures established for the Institution's research publications. Brookings publishes them in the belief that they are worthy of public consideration but does not assume responsibility for their accuracy or objectivity. And, as in all Brookings publications, the judgments, conclusions, and recommendations presented in the Dialogues should not be ascribed to the trustees, officers, or other staff members of the Brookings Institution.

Oil and America's Security

Edited by EDWARD R. FRIED
NANETTE M. BLANDIN

Report of a conference held in Washington, D.C., on October 15, 1987, sponsored by the American Enterprise Institute for Public Policy Research, the Brookings Institution, the Lyndon Baines Johnson Library, and the Lyndon B. Johnson School of Public Affairs at Austin

THE BROOKINGS INSTITUTION / Washington, D.C.

HD
9502
.U52
O54
1988

About Brookings

The Brookings Institution is a private nonprofit organization devoted to research, education, and publication in economics, government, foreign policy, and the social sciences generally. Its principal purpose is to bring knowledge to bear on the current and emerging public policy problems facing the American people. In its research, Brookings functions as an independent analyst and critic, committed to publishing its findings for the information of the public. In its conferences and other activities, it serves as a bridge between scholarship and public policy, bringing new knowledge to the attention of decisionmakers and affording scholars a better insight into policy issues. Its activities are carried out through three research programs (Economic Studies, Government Studies, Foreign Policy Studies), a Center for Public Policy Education, a Publications Program, and a Social Science Computation Center.

The Institution was incorporated in 1927 to merge the Institute for Government Research, founded in 1916 as the first private organization devoted to public policy issues at the national level; the Institute of Economics, established in 1922 to study economic problems; and the Robert Brookings Graduate School of Economics and Government, organized in 1924 as a pioneering experiment in training for public service. The consolidated institution was named in honor of Robert Somers Brookings (1850–1932), a St. Louis businessman whose leadership shaped the earlier organizations.

Brookings is financed largely by endowment and by the support of philanthropic foundations, corporations, and private individuals. Its funds are devoted to carrying out its own research and educational activities. It also undertakes some unclassified government contract studies, reserving the right to publish its findings.

A Board of Trustees is responsible for general supervision of the Institution, approval of fields of investigation, and safeguarding the independence of the Institution's work. The President is the chief administrative officer, responsible for formulating and coordinating policies, recommending projects, approving publications, and selecting staff.

Editors' Preface

Oil has made its mark on the world in the past fifteen years. Two oil price shocks and one price collapse exerted a powerful influence on the world economy and on international relations. Ramifications can be seen in two world recessions, in third world debt problems, as an unspoken presence in attempts to resolve Arab-Israeli differences, in the expansion of the U.S. military role in the Persian Gulf, and in the virulent boom and bust cycles in oil producing countries and in the major oil producing regions in the United States.

Throughout the period, the future course of oil prices and the economic and political consequences have been the subject of intense examination. Views have toned down remarkably as markets have eased. Nonetheless, nervousness persists, stemming principally from the unchallenged fact that the United States and the rest of the oil importing world will become increasingly dependent on oil supplied from the politically troubled Middle East. Does this mean that another oil shock is in our future? Will U.S. security policy become hostage in some respects to our growing oil import dependency? And what can we do to contain damage if oil supplies are seriously interrupted?

To address these questions, a conference was held at the Brookings Institution on October 15, 1987, with speakers, commentators, and participants invited to represent diverse views. The conference was sponsored by the American Enterprise Institute for Public Policy Research, the Brookings Institution, the Lyndon Baines Johnson Library, and the Lyndon B. Johnson School of Public Affairs at Austin. It was planned and organized by Marvin H. Kosters, Nanette M. Blandin, Harry J. Middleton, and Max Sherman, of these sponsoring institutions, respectively. Pamela F. Buckles of Brookings coordinated the conference. Brenda B. Szittya and Caroline Lalire edited the manuscript, and Janet E. Smith prepared it for typesetting.

The editors are grateful to the Lyndon Baines Johnson Foundation for helping to finance the conference.

The views expressed in this volume are those of the authors, commentators, and participants and should not be ascribed to the sponsoring institutions or to their trustees, officers, or other staff members.

August 1988   Edward R. Fried
Washington, D.C.   Nanette M. Blandin

Contents

An Official View

Public Policy Choices

Overview

Some fifteen years of dust has settled since the Organization of Petroleum Exporting Countries' (OPEC) use of the oil weapon and the subsequent oil price shocks raised the link between oil and U.S. security to the level of a major national issue. Successive U.S. administrations sought to grapple with the problem of insulating the nation's economic security and foreign policy from the vagaries of oil supply from the Middle East—the predominant oil producing region in the world and politically the most troubled. Approaches ranged from seeking energy independence for the United States—largely through subsidies to promote energy production and greater efficiency in energy use—to closer international collaboration in energy policy, to reliance on the market to sort everything out. In the end, aspects of all three approaches were embodied in U.S. energy security policy, with the market as the prime mover.

Although uneasiness about this link persists, the issue has long since lost its urgency. Certainly the tenor of the discussion at the conference whose proceedings are reported in this volume provides a sense of proportion about oil security that would have been unusual even as recently as the early 1980s. Then, the question was when, not whether, we would confront the next energy crisis—a crisis usually defined as a replay of past misery. Now, the occurrence of another energy crisis is no longer taken for granted, nor are its consequences defined in near catastrophic terms.

In short, much has been learned about the link between oil and America's security. The propositions that follow attempt to summarize that experience. While these propositions are reflected in the conference discussions, they do not purport to represent the general view or the diversity described in the book.

PAST EXPERIENCE AND FUTURE PROSPECTS

1. The main link between oil and national security is economic. Both in 1973–74 and in 1979–80 political disturbances in the Middle East caused reductions in the world supply of oil. Even though these supply shortfalls were comparatively small, they resulted in very large increases in the price of oil. Because of the economic importance of oil and energy generally, industrial countries found it difficult to absorb these price shocks smoothly. Consequently, world output after each oil price jump was some 6 percent below what it otherwise would have been, until adjustments to the oil price change were completed and trend economic growth resumed.

2. The object of energy security policy is to avoid or mitigate the economic costs of oil supply disruptions. This is not to minimize the constraints that a tight oil market could impose on U.S. foreign policy—a point emphasized by James Schlesinger in opening the conference and subsequently elaborated on by others. In a tight oil market, the argument goes, the United States might decide against policies that otherwise seemed necessary because of the danger that they could touch off an oil supply disruption in retaliation. To be subject to this constraint would undermine the ability of the United States to carry out its responsibilities as a superpower. Oil blackmail in one form or another, however, depends on the size of the economic losses that could result from the withholding of supply, which brings us back to the economic definition of oil security. To the degree these costs can be avoided or mitigated by counteraction, such as the use of emergency oil stocks, the threat of retaliation loses force. In this connection, the experience of the past fifteen years also shows that selective use of the oil weapon is bound to be ineffective and that its general use can ultimately backfire against the oil market interests of the initiators.

3. Whether oil price shocks occur in response to an oil supply interruption depends on the state of the world oil market at that time, not on the degree of U.S. dependency on oil imports. To be sure, the United States is the largest single factor in world oil: U.S. oil consumption is about one-third of the noncommunist world total, and U.S. oil imports are about one-third of world oil trade. Nonetheless, in a world market characterized by substantial excess pro-

duction capacity as at present, prices are slack despite high and rising U.S. oil imports. Even a sizable supply interruption now would not cause prices to escalate anywhere near as much as in the past. By contrast, in a tight market the world economy, including the U.S. economy, would be vulnerable to substantial oil supply disruption costs even if U.S. oil imports were low or declining.

4. Assessing U.S. energy security in isolation is therefore misleading if not dangerous. Mitigating the economic damage from an oil supply interruption will depend on collaborative energy security actions among the OECD (Organization for Economic Cooperation and Development) countries. Together they account for three-fourths of noncommunist oil consumption, and they alone are committed and financially able to hold substantial stocks for use in an emergency. Should these countries work at cross purposes, the effectiveness of the actions of each country, its energy security, and the energy security of all other oil importing countries would be diminished.

5. If an interruption in supplies does not occur, present trends suggest that world oil markets will be comparatively stable through the end of the century. Price jumps or price collapses, while possible, should be of short duration, primarily reflecting pressure tactics by divergent forces within OPEC. U.S. oil imports probably will continue to rise, eventually reaching or exceeding the peak of 8.5 million barrels a day in 1977, as opposed to barely 6 mmbd in 1987. U.S. oil import dependency would then amount to some 50 percent. Nonetheless, excess production capacity in the world would persist, though gradually decline, increasing OPEC's market power. In view of its experience in the 1980s, however, OPEC is likely to use this market power cautiously, so that prices would rise gradually and only modestly in real terms during the 1990s.

6. Although this outlook is essentially comforting, it would still mean that *potential* disruption costs from a sizable supply interruption would grow through the end of the century, that is, with the decline in excess capacity. Indeed, much of this excess capacity, which is concentrated in the Persian Gulf region, could disappear if the supply shortfall was the result of political turmoil or new military conflict in the Middle East, the source of all major oil supply interruptions since 1950.

7. Several helpful changes have taken place since 1979–80, when the events surrounding the Iranian revolution set off the second oil

price shock. The scramble for supply among importers, which exacerbated the pressure on prices in the past, is likely to be less intensive in the future. Operations of the International Energy Agency should result in an improvement in the dissemination of information and in closer international collaboration than existed before. Construction of oil pipelines in the Persian Gulf region would reduce the impact of a disruption of tanker traffic. And the large Persian Gulf producers led by Saudi Arabia would wish to dampen price escalation to avoid damage to future oil markets. Furthermore, at such a time they could well continue to have oil stocks to put on a tightening market and would be prone to do so. Still, the threat of substantial economic damage would exist, making oil security a continuing U.S. and international concern.

POLICY IMPLICATIONS

U.S. administrations since 1973 have been criticized for not having a national energy policy—a concept never carefully defined, but at times seeming to mean support for the particular precepts of the critic regarding energy conservation, energy production, or the preservation of the environment. The Reagan administration's energy policy is equated with exclusive reliance on the market, which is largely, though by no means entirely, true, but in effect it is not much different from the energy policy of previous administrations. To be sure, the U.S. energy past is strewn with price and allocation controls, windfall profit taxes, and subsidies to encourage energy efficiency and the production of alternative fuels. As a whole, those measures were costly—much more so than their effect on dampening price pressures and improving security could justify. Some continue to the present, and rightly. In the end, however, it was the rise in the price of oil from 1973 to 1981—not those measures—that was responsible for the improvements in energy production, interfuel substitution, and efficiency in energy use that eventually eased oil markets and the energy security problem as well. This adjustment also involved large costs in the form of accelerated obsolescence, investments that turned uneconomic, and energy producing regions that were devastated when oil prices fell.

What oil security measures should now be taken given today's outlook for the oil market? The risk of a supply interruption remains uncertain. Should one occur in the next few years, the potential for damage would be quite small. Later in the 1990s this potential will grow, but not on the scale reached in the past crises when the system had no cushion against disruption. In short, the oil future looms less ominously than it once did, suggesting emphasis on comparatively low-cost measures aimed at improving the world market balance, say, ten years from now or at strengthening the world's capacity to contain damage should an interruption occur about that time.

Measures to reduce inefficiency or remove exploration disincentives are evident choices. Repeal of the windfall profit tax on oil, provided in the trade bill signed by the president in August 1988, is an example. The tax had become an anachronism but still served as a disincentive to oil exploration. Completing the deregulation of natural gas would also be useful, not simply because it would increase efficiency but because it would add flexibility to the energy system, strengthening its ability to handle an oil supply disruption.

Beyond these measures, possible U.S. domestic policy actions become more controversial. Most recent attention focuses on the imposition of an oil import fee. Proponents argue that substantial import protection is necessary to avoid further deterioration of the U.S. oil production base, growing import dependency, and constraints on U.S. national security policy decisionmaking. Opponents counter that it makes little sense to accept the substantial economic burden of higher domestic oil prices now for a marginal reduction in the risk of higher prices a decade from now. In other words, costs outweigh security gains.

A variable oil import fee to protect oil exploration investments against the threat of a price collapse is another matter. The fee would go into effect only if prices dropped below a trigger—suggestions range from $10 to $18 a barrel—and would amount at any time to the difference between the trigger price and the market price. Once the market price rose above the trigger price, the import fee would go off. In this case security gains would be modest, but so would costs, if any were incurred.

A settlement needs to be reached on which of the promising U.S. oil and gas areas should be open to exploration. Here energy benefits need to be weighed against environmental costs. Simultaneously blocking the development of the California continental shelf, the

Arctic National Wildlife Refuge, and public lands throughout the West does not seem wise.

There is no disagreement, however, on the cost-effectiveness of the strategic petroleum reserve in providing oil security. U.S. emergency stocks used in close coordination with those of other OECD countries could even now offset a supply interruption of as much as 6 mmbd for six months. This would contain economic damage, provide time to determine what actions were possible to deal with the causes of the oil disruption, and provide protection against attempts by oil exporters to apply foreign policy pressure against the United States. These stocks should be increased through concerted action by the OECD countries. The United States should provide assured financing to accelerate the rate of adding to the reserve and to increase the present goal of 750 million barrels, an increase warranted by the growth in U.S. oil consumption and imports. The United States should use the leverage provided by such action to persuade other countries to build or add to government emergency stocks. Given the present outlook for the oil market, emergency stocks—internationally coordinated—are the most effective line of defense against supply interruptions. Their impact in mitigating the economic damage from a supply interruption would far exceed the security contribution achieved by subsidies of one sort or another to U.S. oil production.

Another way to minimize risks is to take actions that will influence the longer-term supply balance for oil. Included in this category are measures that seek to avoid environmental and other constraints on the use of coal and nuclear energy, to encourage greater efficiency in the use of oil, and to promote alternative fuels so as to make the energy transition less tumultuous. These are spelled out in Congressman Sharp's discussion of practical energy policies—notably public expenditures to develop and demonstrate clean coal technologies, actions to regain public confidence in nuclear energy, and, in general, ways to set objectives for research and development expenditures in the energy field. As always, the policy issue is how to calculate cost-benefit ratios at the margin that can justify a given level of public expenditure for this range of activities.

In sum, the present oil outlook makes it clear that U.S. national security warrants neither crash programs, nor costly programs, nor benign neglect. To be sure, the record shows that medium- and long-term projections of the oil market need to be treated with skepticism. That merely suggests a careful watch on future developments to determine whether a change in direction is necessary. In the meanwhile U.S. oil security policy should center on increasing the buildup of the strategic petroleum reserve and strengthening collaboration with other industrial countries on managing emergencies through the International Energy Agency.

JAMES R. SCHLESINGER

Oil and National Security: An American Dilemma

Until quite recently this nation had no need to worry about its energy supply. From within its own borders the United States could provide the primary energy necessary to satisfy its own requirements and to fulfill its national security obligations, including sustaining its allies during the Suez crisis of 1956. Other great powers—Britain, Germany, Japan—were less fortunate, in a sense, and had to focus early on the linkage between energy and security. By and large, however, Americans did not have to think about this linkage; having to do so now comes hard.

The linkage between security and energy depends on an interplay between economics and security-of-supply considerations. I shall comment first on the economics of energy in this country and then go on to security considerations.

The oil industry in the United States is a classic example of an industry that is unable to stand competition. That proposition has long been recognized by people in the industry, but whether that recognition is implicit or explicit has depended on the price of oil. When oil is in ample supply and prices are depressed, acknowledgement becomes most explicit. Under such circumstances the U.S. industry has strenuously advocated restraint on the inflow of "cheap foreign oil"—a phrase much in vogue thirty years ago and now showing strong signs of revival. Eulogies to a free market and to freedom from government intervention become prominent only when prices are high.

The reason the industry cannot stand unfettered competition is that the production of oil, in contrast to the exploration and development of new resources, is characterized by high fixed costs, low marginal costs, and low labor costs. These characteristics apply to all save the so-called marginal, high-cost wells. The consequence is that under free market conditions supply is inelastic. Moreover, demand is also inelastic in the short run—and fluctuates with economic conditions. When demand contracts or supply expands, prices can plummet. Hence the search for a mechanism of restraint.

Not only has industry sought, but nations have accepted, a requirement for limiting competition. Attending this conference is a former chairman of the Texas Railroad Commission,* as ingenious an instrument for modifying rigorous competition as has ever been designed. It worked effectively to restrain competition within the United States and outside until dominance over the international oil industry departed from our shores. Since that time the OPEC cartel has attempted to serve as a substitute. The absence of such an anti-competitive mechanism, though welcome to consumers, would pose serious problems for American oil production and American security.

Unfettered competition would certainly mean the accelerated decline of U.S. oil production. According to economic theory, in a competitive market it is the marginal producer that sets the price. In today's oil market, curiously enough, it is the intramarginal producer, in fact the lowest-cost oil producer, Saudi Arabia, that determines the price.

Perhaps more important, in a competitive market it is the marginal producer that is subject to being squeezed out. The elegance and the symmetry of the competitive model, first learned in elementary economics, may seem appealing until we suddenly realize that the marginal producer is us, the United States of America. The United States is the world's high-cost producer and increasingly so. The costs of finding, developing, and producing new oil in the United States exceed those in the Persian Gulf by roughly a factor of six. We have the oldest, the most explored, and the most exploited oil provinces in the world. More wells have been drilled in Texas than in the rest of the world combined.

Much of the time, of course, competition will be curtailed through limitations on production by the cartel, limitations that will be welcomed perhaps most notably by fervent supporters of free enterprise. Indeed, those who regularly preach the *philosophy* of free markets for oil production are at the same time beseeching OPEC to

*Mack Wallace. His presentation, "A Perilous Choice: Minesweepers or Drilling Rigs," appears on p. 103. (Ed.)

get its act together to restrict production—and thereby to sustain prices and the American oil industry.

Nevertheless, despite the best efforts of OPEC, there will be a steady decline of U.S. oil production, a prospect that is examined subsequently in this volume. For my purpose it is sufficient to say that at current costs and prices the United States will reach the point of approximately 50 percent oil import dependency, importing some 9 million barrels a day (mmbd), probably by the end of 1990. By the middle of the 1990s oil import dependency could rise to the two-thirds level. Oil imports could then amount to 12–13 mmbd—if that much oil turns out to be available.

Any attempt to protect high-cost producers through departure from free market conditions involves costs, which in this case have to be paid by consumers or taxpayers. Are such costs worth paying? Adam Smith, reputedly the high priest of free markets, whose face adorns the neckties of Reagan administration stalwarts, asserted quite clearly and pungently, "Defense is more important than opulence." If he were to survey U.S. oil policy today, Adam Smith might well ask: "Do we care whether American oil production is on an accelerated decline? Is it a trend sufficiently important to the United States to be worth paying to prevent or to mitigate?"

As noted, by the end of 1990 the United States will be importing a record 9 mmbd. U.S. oil consumption is once again expanding, at an annual rate of 300,000 to 400,000 barrels a day. Domestic oil production is down by 1.1 mmbd from the level achieved in February 1986. In the lower forty-eight states, production has been dropping at the rate of 30,000 barrels a day each month. In a year or so a decline will finally set in on the North Slope in Alaska. Does the United States really care? Is it prepared to live with the consequences of rising oil consumption and declining production?

An argument can be made that the United States should not be overconcerned about domestic production. It will be obliged in any event to sustain the lifeline to the Persian Gulf—as part of its overall strategy to preserve the free world. To put it differently, the United States is itself no longer an island but an integral part of the world oil market. It is access to that market, not the growing degree of U.S. oil import dependency, that matters. Why pay more for additional insurance?

The Reagan administration itself behaves as if free markets provide the appropriate guide for policy. To be sure, it did waffle a bit in

1986 under the pressure of the oil price collapse. But that waffling apparently reflected domestic political conditions—the disaffection of Republican eagles down in the oil patch—more than it did doubts about the wisdom of relying on the free market backed up by the strategic petroleum reserve.

I believe the United States should be worried. Its role in the world is unique. Unlike Germany, Japan, or France, all of which, incidentally, worry a great deal about oil dependency, the United States is the great stabilizing power in the free world. Other nations can be oil dependent. If, however, the United States is to sustain its role in the world and to maintain the necessary freedom of action in foreign policy matters, it cannot afford to become excessively dependent on oil imports, particularly from the most volatile regions of the world.

A review of recent history will serve to illustrate my point.

The oil problem has been more or less coterminous with the problems of the Middle East. In 1956 the Israelis, with the support (and the connivance) of the British and French, invaded Egypt and advanced toward the Suez Canal, with the intent that their European allies recover that waterway. At that time the United States had sufficient shut-in oil capacity to export oil to Britain and France, replacing supplies lost from the Middle East. The implicit U.S. threat to cut off that oil augmented the diplomatic pressures the United States was bringing to bear on the British and French to terminate the invasion of the canal zone.

In 1958 the United States introduced its forces into Lebanon, more successfully, I might add, than in its more recent involvement. In 1958 it could do so without any apprehension regarding the security of its oil supply.

By 1967 the United States had become a modest net importer of oil. During the Arab-Israeli Six-Day War there was a nominal cutoff of some Middle Eastern oil to the United States. Import dependency, however, was sufficiently low to allow the United States to disregard both the nominal embargo and the intended diplomatic pressure.

By 1973 U.S. policy leeway had narrowed substantially—perhaps more than we then recognized—because of the growth in U.S. oil import dependency. By that time, subsequent to the report of the Shultz Committee,[1] the Nixon administration had abandoned the

1. See Cabinet Task Force on Oil Import Control, *The Oil Import Question: A Report on the Relationship of Oil Imports to the National Security* (Government

Eisenhower-era effort to limit oil imports (initially to 12 percent of domestic requirements). Dependence on the Middle East had become significant. No one, certainly not the producing states, fully anticipated the consequences of the oil embargo that commenced after the United States started to resupply Israel with military equipment in October. Whatever else may be said, that action captured America's (and the world's) attention.

Since 1973 uncertainty about the world oil market has grown. The panicky reactions in the oil-importing countries at the time of the Arab oil embargo in 1973 and then again after the Iranian revolution in 1978 have remained a perennial source of concern. Despite the substantial unused production capacity around the world at the outset of the Iran-Iraq war in 1980, another panicky reaction ensued. It has taken considerable time for the buildup of surplus capacity around the world to exercise its influence and for the market to settle down to reflect the prevailing balance between the supply of and demand for oil. Today the ebb and flow of the tanker war in the Gulf has remarkably little impact on the oil market. Would that be the case in the absence of substantial excess capacity?

Let me close this historical review by citing two telling examples that suggest the influence of oil market conditions on national security policy. In April 1986 the president of the United States ordered an attack on Tripoli to punish Colonel Muammar Qadhafi for his encouragement of terrorism. It is not my purpose to examine the merits of that decision. Some may disapprove; others may be enthusiastic. My purpose here is simply to emphasize this crucial fact: the freedom that the United States enjoyed to undertake this measure was to a large degree a reflection of conditions in the oil market— slack pricing and substantial excess capacity. If instead the United States had faced a tight oil market and if it had been heavily dependent on imported oil, much of it from the Middle East, it is not clear to me that the United States would have felt sufficiently free to take that step. Certainly the policy leeway available to a president to do so would have been greatly circumscribed. And even more certainly that policy leeway will become more circumscribed in the future. Thus a tight oil market probably means the recrudescence of the oil

Printing Office, 1970). George P. Shultz, then secretary of labor, chaired the committee.

weapon, at least in the eyes of the major players in the Middle East.

Finally, let me touch on the example of the current U.S. actions in the Persian Gulf. To be sure, it is not altogether clear to me what the United States is doing in the Persian Gulf—or why it is there in such force. But it is clear that it has something to do with our concern about oil supply. The United States has moved some 40 ships and 25,000 men to the Persian Gulf to face down the pressures emanating from Ayatollah Khomeini. Would the United States have been prepared to act so vigorously if the world oil market were tight, if the nation were 55 or 60 percent dependent on foreign sources of supply, and if moving into the Persian Gulf were likely to cause a jump in oil prices at least in the short run? After all, the price of gasoline at the pump is one of the politically most sensitive pressure points in American life. Would a U.S. administration be prepared to let the pump price go up? Would it do so in an election year?

The solutions to our national problem with oil, if we choose to use them, are at hand and are well understood. They are to encourage overall energy conservation, especially of oil; to promote the development and use of domestic energy resources; and to substitute other energy resources for imported oil. There is nothing complex about the strategy, but it does involve both some cost and some adjustment in the economy.

In contrast, the administration's oil policy has, by and large, been guided by this advice from Scripture: "Take therefore no thought for the morrow; for the morrow shall take thought for the things of itself. Sufficient unto the day is the evil thereof."

Discussion

Max Sherman asked what specific measures might be adopted to increase the use of domestic primary energy resources and reduce oil import dependency.

Schlesinger's first recommendation was to use the tax code to encourage U.S. oil exploration and development. Since the industry has been dependent on tax subsidies for many years in order to compete with foreign oil, Schlesinger preferred using tax subsidies to interfering with the price mechanism. Specifically, he favored a variable depletion allowance to provide stonger government support for exploration and development activities.

Further, he said, the government has a role in helping the industry to cope with ongoing market volatility. The near term is filled with problems for the oil industry. Iraq will be able to put more oil on the market because of the completion of a new pipeline to Turkey and an additional line through Saudi Arabia to Yanbu. Iran is exploring the possibility of sending oil to the Soviet Union, for export, by altering the gas pipeline to that country. And North Yemen may soon be exporting 200,000 barrels a day. All this additional oil will be difficult for the oil market to absorb quickly.

To help stabilize the U.S. industry in the face of this volatility, Schlesinger would consider government subsidies for oil production when the price falls below $15 to $18 a barrel. After all, if a tax on oil was warranted when the price rose to $40 a barrel, subsidies to production could be warranted when the price falls below $15 to $18 a barrel. He would be reluctant to move in the direction of a fixed oil import fee, which in his view would eventually bring about a return to the entitlement system. Instead, he would advocate establishing a floor price of $15 to $18 a barrel, which would protect oil exploration activities against another collapse in price. At that level, it probably would go into effect for only brief periods, because OPEC is likely to be able, by and large, to sustain the price of $18 a barrel. Such a floor price would be similar to the minimum safeguard price of $7 a barrel, adjusted for inflation, that the International Energy Agency (IEA) adopted in 1975 to encourage domestic energy production in its member countries. A minimum, or floor, price, furthermore, would not be seen by consumers, and hence voters, as increasing the price of oil, which is an important political consideration.

Charles Stalon asked whether Schlesinger favored subsidies to encourage production of alternative energy supplies so as to limit the demand for oil?

Schlesinger said he would be inclined to encourage American industry to turn to alternatives other than oil through the use of the government's powers of persuasion, which are substantial, but at the same time minimize the direct role of government.

One area that needs straightening out, he said, is the incredible mess in the U.S. nuclear power industry. American technology is being well exploited by the Japanese, the French, and others, as they move to reliance on nuclear power for 50 to 60 percent of their electric power production, but it is no longer being used at all for new capacity in the United States.

Furthermore, the natural gas resource base is underutilized and should be more extensively exploited. Of course, if we produce more oil or more gas now, we will run out of it sooner. But in terms of the U.S. power position in the world, it is so important to get through the next forty or fifty years that it is worth running the risk of what might happen in the more distant future. The United States faces clear and present dangers and should deal with them.

Donna Fitzpatrick asked three questions: Is there a world beyond oil? What do we want it to look like? And how do we get there?

Schlesinger replied that in public policy terms these questions brought to the fore the role of research and development in the United States. How much should we be spending for solar energy development and for other future alternative energy sources? He believes the United States spent too much for these purposes in the 1970s and is not spending enough today.

The shape of the world beyond oil is difficult, if not impossible, to define at present. Natural gas will be around a good deal longer than oil, particularly in the North American continent. Beyond oil and natural gas, there will be a period in which gassified coal or hydrogen may be the power source for automobiles. We will increasingly turn to electric power, for which there will be a return of nuclear energy in its fission form and later in the form of fusion. The role of the Department of Energy in providing for appropriate levels of research and development is therefore an extremely important one. Regrettably, budget pressure will make it difficult to sustain R&D at an appropriate level.

The U.S. government should not commit itself to major federal support for production. That goes beyond its legitimate role. On the other hand, the government has an appropriate role in creating prototype facilities, such as the facility to produce synthetic gas in the Great Plains. When the price of oil rises and the industry becomes interested, a prototype will be ready. That should be the end of the federal government's responsibility. Going to the prototype stage, however, is beyond what the Reagan administration is inclined to do, preferring instead to confine activities to R&D narrowly defined.

Jeffrey Jones pointed out that the 1979–80 oil shock was in part an inventory phenomenon and that future military upheavals could cause similar shocks. Stocks therefore are critical. He asked what might be done to prevent commercial firms from using the increase in government stocks as an excuse to reduce their normal inventories.

Schlesinger had no easy answer. For one thing, he believes the target for the U.S. strategic petroleum reserve should be larger than the present 750 million barrels. That amount might do when imports are 4 mmbd but would be inadequate when daily imports rise to 10 mmbd. Government jawboning might also help, but as of now Schlesinger would not be prepared to call for regulations requiring the industry to maintain a given amount of supply in relation to imports.

It is true, he said, that in 1979–80 and even to some extent in 1973, the impact on the oil market was grossly disproportionate to the actual physical shortage of oil. The reason was panic. At the least, prudent action by firms to expand their oil inventories is likely to be a feature of future emergencies. In 1979 the United States discouraged companies from a scramble to build stocks, as it was obligated to do in accordance with the pledges given to the IEA, but equivalent restraint was not exercised by the Germans and the Japanese, who were buying up as much oil as they could. Then consumers began to panic and began trying to keep their gasoline tanks full, which added to the pressure on supply. This kind of panic or prudential action drives the energy crisis during supply interruption, and it simply must be taken as a fact of life that has to be addressed.

Salvatore Lazzari asked whether Schlesinger favored a variable oil import fee and whether, like the fixed oil import fee, it would be likely to create pressure for the reestablishment of entitlements?

Schlesinger replied that pressure for entitlements will come as soon as the price of domestic oil is significantly above the international level. If a variable import fee establishes an appropriate floor price, he would favor it as a means of preventing the American oilmen in western Texas and southern Louisiana from thinking that they may face $9 a barrel oil.

Frank Wolf asked what measures the government should take to encourage conservation and, specifically, whether fuel efficiency standards for automobiles were appropriate.

Schlesinger said he was in full agreement with President Carter's statement that "conservation is the cornerstone of the national energy policy." At the time of Carter's comment, there was a good deal of scoffing, because of the belief—later proved wrong—that energy consumption and economic growth marched in lockstep. The great engine for conservation, of course, was the OPEC price increase, but preachments of government have an important role to play.

The Reagan administration first took its position from the 1980 statements of the president to the effect that conservation means being hot in summer and cold in winter. It has now begun to preach conservation but is reluctant to impose conservation standards on industry. As to fuel efficiency standards in the automobile industry, the problem at the moment is not to impose new standards but to sustain those already on the books.

Christopher Flavin commented that improved energy efficiency largely created the oil glut that now exists and that the potential for further gain remains large. More than preaching is required on the part of the administration. There are still actions to be taken, particularly in regard to the building and automobile industries, to save energy. If we look at the next twenty years and the need to reduce import dependence, should not the priority be placed on addressing the poor energy efficiency performance in those areas?

Schlesinger replied that he takes conservation for granted and that improving energy efficiency has been national policy on and off since the early 1970s. But building codes are under the jurisdiction of local governments and not much political force for efficiency gains exists there. We should continue to try, while recognizing that the prospects for success are limited.

The United States has a long-term energy problem, and we ought to deal with that by moving toward more fuel-efficient systems. It also has a short-term energy problem: oil consumption is going up, and oil production in the United States is going down. To say that the United States must deal first with the short-term problem does not in any way lessen the need to use energy efficiently over the long term.

Energy conservation by the Europeans and the Japanese since 1979 has been more impressive than it has been in the United States.

Indeed, the United States is moving toward consuming 35 percent of world oil production. At the next increase in oil prices, the United States will again be charged as being the greatest squanderer of energy. It should be taking measures now to avoid that, simply by accomplishing the kinds of things that the Japanese and the Europeans have already accomplished.

Schlesinger further pointed out that in fact conservation has not been the most important cause of the slack oil market. Oil consumption worldwide is now about 10 percent below what it was in 1979–80. The most important reason for the slack in the oil market is the 5 mmbd of non-OPEC production that was brought on by the price increase. If the increase in non-OPEC production is reversed in the future, the present oil glut will rapidly diminish.

Jacques Maroni commented that making vehicles significantly more efficient does not necessarily conserve energy unless the price of fuel also increases. The per mile automobile fuel cost today is lower than it has been for many years, which encourages the dispersion of population and a more than proportionate increase in the number of miles driven. Fuel efficiency is up, but the use of gasoline has also increased. The latter will not decline unless the cost of fuel rises. As a means to reduce oil consumption, he asked about the merits of taxing refiner use of imported oil, which would raise the cost of gasoline while encouraging domestic oil production.

Schlesinger agreed that greater automobile fuel efficiency tends to reduce fuel costs and thus encourage driving. Although greater efficiency would not save on gas consumption, it might still be a benefit to society as a whole. He did not place great emphasis on fuel efficiency standards as such, preferring instead to achieve the same objective through the price mechanism. For that reason, he had favored a tax on "gas guzzlers," arguing that people should be able to own them if they were prepared to pay to do so.

As for a gasoline tax, Schlesinger emphasized that the problem is political; no price is more sensitive in the United States than that of gasoline. The Carter administration initially proposed a tax of 50 cents a gallon on gasoline in 1977, which the Senate did not even bother to consider. Although the request was substantially reduced, the administration still could not gain the support of Congress. A refiner tax on imported oil would suffer the same disadvantages, while also raising the threat of a return to entitlements.

Energy Trends Through the 1990s

CHARLES J. DiBONA

Long-Term Trends in Oil Markets

The dramatic developments in world oil markets over the past two years have had far-reaching effects both in the United States and abroad. The United States, which is the world's largest oil importer, has benefited from the sharp fall in oil prices since late 1985. Because the average price of crude oil dropped about $13 a barrel in 1986, the U.S. oil import bill fell about $16 billion despite a more than 400 million barrel increase in volume. This saving is equal to about one-half of one percent of U.S. gross national product.

But not all the news has been good. The oil price fall has also created serious problems that have not been adequately recognized by U.S. policymakers. Specifically, it has set in motion forces that, if unchecked, will substantially increase an already large U.S. dependence on oil imports.

This paper discusses likely trends in U.S. and world oil markets, examines some implications of increased U.S. reliance on OPEC oil, which now seems to be inevitable, and suggests in broad outline public policies that can improve U.S. energy security.

RESPONSES TO OIL PRICE CHANGES

To assess the course of oil markets over the next decade, it is helpful to review some recent history. After rising sharply during the 1970s, the price of oil peaked at $37 a barrel in 1981, declined steadily thereafter to $27 a barrel by 1985, and then plummeted to $14 a barrel in 1986.[1] Although the price rose somewhat in 1987, it still was far

1. Prices represent annual averages of U.S. refiner acquisition costs for imported crude oil. U.S. Department of Energy, Energy Information Administration, *Monthly Energy Review* (August 1987). Unless otherwise noted, oil data for the United States cited in this paper are from publications of U.S. Department of Energy, Energy Information Administration. Data for other countries are from publications of the International Energy Agency.

below the levels of the early 1980s. Indeed, after adjustment for inflation, the October 1987 price was below the price reached after the first oil price shock of 1973–74.

Reactions to the price hikes of the 1970s were dramatic. As oil consumption fell and production rose in the United States, imports of oil were cut from 8.8 million barrels a day in 1977 to 5.1 mmbd in 1985, more than 40 percent. Moreover, studies have shown that consumer and producer responses to higher oil prices would have been even greater had it not been for federal price controls, which held prices of domestically produced crude oil and oil products significantly below the world price until after 1981.[2] In addition, the so-called windfall profit tax of 1980 continued to prevent U.S. oil producers from obtaining the full benefits of the world price. The American Petroleum Institute estimates that U.S. crude oil production today would be almost 1 mmbd higher had the windfall tax not been enacted.

In the non-OPEC, noncommunist countries outside the United States, oil consumption showed little net change between 1973 and 1979, falling during the 1974–75 recession and then rising. After the second price jump in 1979, however, consumption declined substantially through 1985. On the supply side, oil production rose markedly as important new sources of oil were developed in OECD countries, such as the United Kingdom and Norway, as well as in non-OPEC developing countries, such as Mexico and Egypt. In all, between 1979 and 1985, production rose about 5 mmbd while consumption fell 5 mmbd in this group of countries.

Thus demand and supply responses to the 1970s oil price hikes were pronounced. They were also unanticipated. Many people in government, the media, and industry simply did not expect them. And now, as then, many policymakers seem to be underestimating the likely responses to oil price changes—this time to lower oil prices.

The fall in world oil prices that began in 1981 was a direct result of the changes in the net oil position of the non-OPEC countries that the two OPEC price shocks had brought about. As oil consumption in the United States and in other non-OPEC countries declined while production rose, demand for oil from OPEC, the residual supplier

2. See Joseph P. Kalt, *The Economics and Politics of Oil Price Regulation in the Post-Embargo Era* (MIT Press, 1981).

whose members hold about three-quarters of the noncommunist world's oil reserves, dropped sharply. Between 1979 and 1985 OPEC had to cut production almost 50 percent, about 15 mmbd. Even this large cut in OPEC production could not prevent the price of oil from slipping. Saudi Arabia, which had been the "swing" producer within the OPEC group and had drastically reduced its output between 1981 and 1985, abandoned that role in late 1985. It increased production, and the price of oil fell abruptly by more than $10 a barrel in January 1986.

U.S. oil consumption and production have responded sharply to the price drop. Consumption in 1987 has been about 300,000 barrels a day higher than in 1986, and about 800,000 barrels a day higher than in 1985. By late 1987 oil production including natural gas liquids was down about 1.1 mmbd from its February 1986 peak.

As a result, U.S. oil imports rose more than 1.1 mmbd in 1986, or 23 percent. This trend continues. In the first eight months of 1987 imports were about 400,000 barrels a day, or 7 percent, above their level in the first eight months of 1986. Oil imports as a percentage of total U.S. oil consumption are rapidly approaching 48 percent, the all-time high reached in 1977.

U.S. oil production is not likely to improve soon. Drilling activity fell sharply during 1986, accelerating the downward trend that began in 1981. The number of oil and gas well completions fell more than 30,000, or by nearly one-half, the largest annual decline on record. This decline continued in 1987. All this does not augur well for future U.S. oil production, since the reserves needed to maintain production are not being found and developed. Indeed, in 1986 the United States replaced less than half of the crude oil reserves it used up. And because of the several-year lag in many areas between decisions to invest and the beginning of commercial production, U.S. oil production will be slow to recover when world oil prices rise in the future.

Lower oil prices have also affected oil consumption and production outside the United States. Non-U.S. free world consumption was up about 2 percent in 1987, compared with an average annual decline of about 1 percent during the previous four years. And consumption in the first half of this year was up about 1 percent from a year earlier. On the supply side, although oil production in free world, non-OPEC nations outside the United States was stable in 1986 and

TABLE 1. *U.S. Oil Supply-Demand Balance, 1985, and Projected, 1990, 1995, 2000*

Millions of barrels a day

Item	1985	1990	1995	2000
High-price case				
Consumption	15.7	16.3	17.0	17.4
Domestic supply[a]	11.5	10.1	9.1	8.3
Net imports	4.2	6.2	7.9	9.1
Low-price case				
Consumption	15.7	17.6	19.0	19.9
Domestic supply[a]	11.5	9.2	7.6	6.3
Net imports	4.2	8.4	11.4	13.6

Source: National Petroleum Council, *Factors Affecting U.S. Oil and Gas Outlook* (NPC, 1987).

a. Includes crude oil and natural gas liquids production, processing gain, inventory changes, and synthetic liquids production.

up moderately in 1987, this increase was far smaller than the average 8 percent annual gain during 1981–85.

FUTURE TRENDS

The American Petroleum Institute has reviewed a number of private and government forecasts of future energy trends. The projections presented below, which have been prepared by the National Petroleum Council (NPC), a private sector group that advises the U.S. Department of Energy, are typical of these forecasts.

The NPC assesses two alternative oil price paths. Its high-price case assumes that the inflation-adjusted price of oil will rise 5 percent annually, starting at $19 a barrel in 1987, close to the actual price. Its low-price case assumes that the real price of oil will rise 4 percent annually, starting at $13 a barrel in 1987. Although $13 seems low, the experience of 1986 indicates that prices in this range are not as farfetched as they once would have seemed.

Under both price scenarios, the demand for oil is expected to grow in the noncommunist world, while non-OPEC oil production is projected to decline. As shown in table 1, U.S. oil production is

TABLE 2. *Non-U.S., Noncommunist World Oil Supply-Demand Balance, 1985, and Projected, 1990, 1995, 2000*
Millions of barrels a day

Item	1985	1990	1995	2000
High-price case				
Consumption	30.7	31.9	33.5	35.0
Non-OPEC production	14.6	15.3	15.6	15.0
Low-price case				
Consumption	30.7	33.4	35.7	38.0
Non-OPEC Production	14.6	14.0	13.7	13.1

Source: See table 1.

TABLE 3. *Demand for OPEC Oil, 1985, and Projected, 1990, 1995, 2000*
Millions of barrels a day

Item	1985	1990	1995	2000
High-price case	17.2	20.6	24.0	27.5
Low-price case	17.2	25.8	31.8	37.0

Source: See table 1.

expected to be particularly hard hit in the low-price case, since the United States is a relatively high-cost producer. In the low-price scenario, U.S. petroleum liquids production would fall to 7.6 mmbd in 1995, or only 40 percent of expected total U.S. oil consumption, and to 6.3 mmbd in the year 2000, or only 32 percent of consumption. Even in the high-price case, domestic supply is expected to be less than half of total consumption by 2000. It should be emphasized that these projections are based on the price assumptions that were outlined above. They are not forecasts of what will actually happen.

Non-OPEC production outside the United States is expected to be roughly stable in the high-price case and to fall moderately in the low-price case (table 2). Non-U.S. oil consumption is expected to increase substantially in both cases.

The NPC projects rapid increases in total demand for oil from the OPEC member nations. Demand in the year 2000 is projected at 27.5 mmbd in the high-price case and 37 mmbd in the low-price case (table 3). On these projections, demand for OPEC oil by the year

2000 would be at least 50 percent higher than, and probably as much as double, the 1985 level.

IMPLICATIONS OF INCREASING RELIANCE ON OPEC OIL

Greater reliance on OPEC oil has important economic implications for the United States and other oil-importing nations. First, higher demand for that oil will tend to raise the world oil price. Oil prices have risen significantly when demand for OPEC oil has absorbed more than 80 percent of OPEC capacity (current capacity is about 27 mmbd), and prices have risen especially sharply when demand exceeded 90 percent of OPEC capacity, which might well occur within just a few years.

On the basis of the historical relation between OPEC capacity utilization and price changes, a 1 mmbd change in the demand for OPEC oil would have a profound effect on importing countries. For example, assuming an initial price of between $15 and $25 a barrel, an increase in demand of 1 mmbd is estimated to raise the world price by $1 to $2 a barrel if the OPEC capacity utilization rate is 80 percent, and by some $5 to $9 a barrel if OPEC capacity utilization is 90 percent.

Greater reliance on OPEC oil not only will tend to raise world oil prices but also will make the importing nations more vulnerable to a supply disruption—not an implausible event in the Middle East. By raising oil prices sharply and suddenly, a supply disruption transfers wealth from oil-importing to oil-exporting nations. In addition, there are sizable indirect costs. A large supply disruption of, say, 10 mmbd could reduce U.S. gross national product by as much as 7 percent.[3]

What might change the outlook? Certainly, changes in U.S. policy affecting energy could make some difference, both with regard to oil consumption and production. But there are limits to what can be done. The petroleum industry is inherently cyclical; the cycles probably cannot or should not be eliminated. At best, the government

3. For example, see Henry S. Rowen and John P. Weyant, "Reducing the Economic Impacts of Oil Supply Disruptions: An International Perspective," *Energy Journal* (January 1982).

can dampen them. For the most part, it has made them and their consequences worse.

Analysts generally do not believe that at any reasonably expected price the United States could increase its oil production significantly, although with a sufficient price increase it probably could maintain the current level for a while. Demand increases can be limited, but it is reasonable to expect some rise in imports. What can be done is to buy time for the country to work out longer-term solutions—but that can happen only if there are better laws, rules, and regulatory actions than are now in place.

The oil industry has a simple agenda for government action: remove impediments to U.S. production. Eliminating the so-called windfall profit tax, which actually is an excise tax on domestically produced oil, ending price controls on natural gas, and opening government land, especially in Alaska and offshore, would help— and certainly be consistent with letting the free play of market forces work.

Currently, a Senate-House conference is considering repeal of the windfall profit tax as part of the trade bill approved by Congress.* Repeal is in the interest of consumers in all regions of the country, simply because it would stimulate domestic oil production, reduce demand for OPEC oil, and thus put downward pressure on world oil prices. Since Americans consume about 6 billion barrels of oil annually, even a relatively small oil price reduction such as $1 a barrel would reduce oil costs to U.S. consumers by about $6 billion a year. And if OPEC is operating at over 80 percent of its capacity, repeal of the windfall profit tax would probably produce much greater savings—perhaps as much as $30 billion a year nationally—because the additional U.S. production would probably restrain OPEC from increasing prices as much. In any event, the savings to consumers in oil costs are likely to far exceed the tax revenues forgone by the federal government. The American Petroleum Institute estimates that the consumer savings will be one-and-a-half to three times as great as the forgone federal revenues.

Congress is also considering whether to open up the Arctic National Wildlife Refuge for oil exploration and development. Much may be

*The president signed a revised trade bill on August 23, 1988, which included a provision repealing the windfall profit tax on oil. (Ed.)

gained and little is to be lost by permitting leasing and exploration. If commercially producible discoveries are not made, petroleum activities will cease, there will be no appreciable risk of environmental damage, and the land will be restored. If commercial finds are made, the national benefits could be enormous; the area may contain a super-giant field comparable to Alaska's Prudhoe Bay, which has been providing 15 to 20 percent of all the oil produced in the United States since 1977. And the petroleum industry's record in developing and producing fields on the Alaska North Slope proves that such operations can be and are being conducted in an environmentally sound manner.

In sum, there is a growing dependence on OPEC supplies in the United States and worldwide. Within a few years, an increase in demand for those supplies probably will cause sharp rises in price with consequent economic and possibly political disruptions.

These problems cannot be entirely avoided. The marginal supply of oil is concentrated in one small part of the world, and it is an unstable area. The United States and other importers of oil could, however, take steps to ameliorate the economic damage from future energy shocks and to buy time to find solutions. The question is whether they will understand the danger and act soon enough.

Considering past performance, there are valid grounds for skepticism. The one glimmer of hope is that there is a growing recognition of the problem by a small but important part of American society—some academicians, editorial writers, spokesmen for energy-using industries, and political leaders. To the extent that their insight can be converted into a broader appreciation of the danger, it could form the basis for an improved national energy policy.

HENDRIK S. HOUTHAKKER

Factors Shaping Long-Term Oil Markets

I will introduce my comments with a brief remark on the present oil scene. Sending a large fleet to the Persian Gulf is one of the best investments the U.S. government has made. It has more than paid for itself. Since the fleet arrived in the Gulf, the price of oil has fallen about $2 to $3 a barrel, which amounts to a saving of about $15 million a day for the U.S. economy. By press accounts, keeping the fleet there costs only $3 million a day, so the investment is earning a handsome return. This action underlines an important fact about the oil market—it is highly unstable, both politically and economically. So far at least, intervention of the U.S. fleet in the Gulf has had favorable political and economic consequences.

Turning to the main subject of this paper, the longer-run factors in the world market, I will first discuss market trends, then examine the problems of exploration, and finally offer some policy suggestions.

MARKET TRENDS

I think the most noteworthy point is that the market system in oil works pretty well. It does not work perfectly, but it works well enough—certainly better than it did twenty years ago, when I first began examining oil policy problems. In part, this improvement is attributable to the introduction of new mechanisms, the most important of which is the futures market. Once a futures market is established, it tends to dominate pricing in an industry; this is happening now in oil. The futures markets in crude oil and in products have been successful and have had a major impact. That does not mean they can stabilize the price of oil. What futures markets do essentially is to substitute short-run instability for long-run instability.

Futures markets tend to be jumpy. Whenever there is news, good or bad, the market exaggerates it, at least for a few days, but then comes to its senses. Some players lose, some gain—but eventually the market finds the right level. That is very different from the situation twenty years ago, when the federal and state agencies were heavily involved in oil price policy and on the whole did not do very well.

As to the demand for oil as a factor shaping the longer-run outlook, the point to stress is the existence of price elasticity, a point that has been amply demonstrated in recent years. In 1974 many in the industry tended to discount this phenomenon, particularly as it applied to gasoline, but now its force is widely understood. Elasticity of oil demand with respect to income also exists and at times works in different directions from price elasticity.

Elasticity of oil supply in respect to price has also proved to be significant, as Jim Schlesinger has reminded us. In recent years oil production outside of OPEC expanded substantially, probably by more than the 5 million barrels a day he mentioned. That figure apparently excludes new production in the Soviet Union and China. It is unfortunate that production developments in those countries are usually excluded from such analyses, since what happens there figures prominently in the world picture.

Indeed, the Soviet Union is by far the world's largest oil producer, with an output of nearly 13 million barrels a day. It is also one of the world's largest exporters, despite its huge domestic consumption. There have been times in recent years when the Soviet Union was the second largest exporter in the world after Saudi Arabia. The Soviet Union's performance is especially remarkable because the bulk of its increase in production has come from areas in which no oil was produced ten years ago; namely, in very inhospitable parts of Siberia. Questions are always raised about whether the Soviets can keep this production up. The Central Intelligence Agency has a long history of gloomy stories about how Soviet oil wells are running down and how Soviet production is peaking and on the road to decline. Yet so far these forecasts have proved to be incorrect.

China also has produced substantially more oil in recent years, though again most of it is consumed domestically. Nevertheless, if China goes on expanding its oil industry at anything like the rate achieved in 1986–87, it may also become an important exporter.

Basically there is only one world oil market, and it does not make any serious distinction between communist oil and noncommunist oil. The convention of including only net exports from communist countries in world oil market statistics while excluding production and consumption data for these countries may be unduly confining as a basis for speculating about future market trends.

EXPLORATION

Exploration is the key to sustained production in the future. In this connection, I see little need to worry about "the world after oil." The world is unlikely to run out of oil before the middle of the twenty-third century; it is not something that present policy can do much to influence. Oil is going to be with us for a long, long time, although it may decline as a proportion of total energy and may have to be reserved for its most important uses. In any event, concern about a world after oil has no proper place on the present policy agenda.

Although prospects for continuing use and reliance on oil are good, exploration is necessary to realize them. And exploration has suffered in various parts of the world, especially in the United States and Canada, from the temporary effects of the oil price collapse that occurred in the first half of 1986. That price collapse hit some firms hard, with quite a few going bankrupt. The failures created an impression that the industry as a whole was in deep trouble. But that is hardly the case, either in the United States or anywhere else.

The present price of oil is still very high by historical standards. As recently as 1971 the U.S. domestic price of oil was less than $3.50 a barrel, or about $10 or $12 in today's dollars. The present price of oil is still almost twice as high in real terms. Twenty years ago was a period of high U.S. domestic production, too high in my view. It was also a period of considerable exploration. There is no reason that this should not be true today. The costs of producing and finding oil have risen much less than the increase in prices. Once the industry has adjusted to the temporary losses it has suffered, it will again find and produce oil in line with earlier experience, except for some extremely high-cost oil wells.

Consequently, some optimism about exploration in the United States is justified. Activity is extending to new areas, though no one can know where oil in fact will be found. Petroleum geology is more an art than a science, and some large discoveries of the past two decades have come in surprising places. These discoveries have led to new thinking about exploration, which in turn will lead to new finds, some of which will be in the United States, others in nearby areas.

A more serious matter than diminished exploration in the United States, which will recover, is the lack of exploration by the members of OPEC. Exploration in those countries is low primarily because further discoveries would make the cartel's effort to control oil prices much more difficult. In some countries, notably Saudi Arabia, reserves are already huge. Kuwait, another country with large oil reserves, set out to drill for gas for local consumption and by accident found another huge oil field. Such stories are indicative of the amount of oil still to be found in the Middle East. These countries for the most part have little or no incentive to search actively for oil and are not likely to do so until the market outlook changes. Fortunately, however, some new producers in the area are not members of OPEC. North Yemen, an important example, has found a lot of oil and will undoubtedly find more because it appears to be in an area of great potential.

Also on the positive side, non-OPEC exploration in general has been very active, with many successes in recent years. Brazil, for instance, which produced a negligible amount of oil ten years ago, now produces half a million barrels a day. By itself that output would not affect the world market a great deal, but Brazil's experience has been repeated in many countries. Together, this new production has been a major cause of the loosening of the world oil market.

U.S. POLICY CONSIDERATIONS

What does this more or less optimistic outlook for world oil resources and supply mean for U.S. energy policies, in particular for tax policies?

A breakdown of OPEC is probably the main risk faced by the U.S. oil industry. OPEC has been the industry's best friend for many years, though not a reliable one because it tends to stumble and fumble from time to time. That is what happened in 1979–80, when

Saudi Arabia lost control of the situation. The cartel overreached itself and prices went too high for reasons that are not entirely clear and in part may have been political. If, instead, OPEC had stuck to the relatively prudent policies it followed after 1973–74 through the period of the Iranian supply interruption, the debacle of 1985–86 would have been avoided. By permitting prices to rise to excess in 1980–81, the cartel paved the way for the later decline of its influence over the world oil market and for the collapse of prices, adversely affecting the U.S. oil industry in the process.

To deal with the risk of another price collapse, the United States should impose a variable fee on imported oil that would go into effect when prices fall below a specified level. That level, or trigger price, should be set low. I have spelled out the case for such a variable oil-import fee in another paper.[1] Such a fee could give the U.S. oil industry some insurance against the recurrence of a price collapse in the future, one in which the price of oil might approach $5 a barrel. In my view, that is the only risk for which the industry needs government protection.

In theory, a tariff could be used to capture some of the monopoly profits of OPEC. In practice, though this possibility existed at the end of the 1970s, I do not believe it exists now. It could not be effectively imposed by the United States alone. A fixed tariff put into effect by the OECD countries together probably could eliminate a large part of OPEC's monopoly profits. Such an effort, however, would require an unprecedented level of cooperation and diplomacy among the OECD countries. It is inconceivable that the Japanese or the French would take part; the British might be anxious to do so and the Germans might be interested, but other countries might not be willing to go along. A fixed tariff does not, therefore, have any merit in itself.

In general, U.S. policy should not be geared to the notion that oil production in the United States is too low. On the contrary, I believe it can be argued that production in the United States is currently too high. One example is production from the naval petroleum reserves, the source of the notorious Teapot Dome scandal during the admin-

1. Hendrik S. Houthakker, *The Ups and Downs of Oil*, in Philip Cagan, ed., *Deficits, Taxes, and Economic Adjustments* (Washington, D.C.: American Enterprise Institute, 1987), pp. 153–80.

istration of President Harding. At present, the naval reserve at Elk Hills, California, is producing at a high rate. Yet there is no reason that reserves established for national security reasons should be used in this way when there is no national security need.

I believe this policy demands rethinking. What is needed in the United States, especially for national security reasons, is spare capacity. We should not want our industry to produce all out. If the world is really running out of oil, which I do not believe is true, the United States should conserve its oil, not burn it up now. Keep it for the rainy day that will come sometime in the next century.

Apart from these national security considerations, there are good economic reasons for not producing all out at the moment. The present price is a good one for the industry; it may go higher. There are always surprises, both upside and downside. If the price goes higher, the U.S. oil industry should be in a position to respond with higher production. This reasoning suggests a change of emphasis in our tax system with respect to oil and natural gas. Traditionally the tax system has favored production over exploration: those who found oil were usually given an incentive to produce it. I believe production is no longer the right emphasis. The tax system should encourage people to explore without necessarily taking their find to production. Mechanisms should be devised, best done through the capital markets without direct government involvement, that will encourage the discoverers of some new reserves to keep them out of production.

The oil import program established during the Eisenhower administration allowed for the development and preservation of spare capacity. Under various pressures, however, the notion of spare capacity was gradually abandoned. By the late 1960s spare capacity no longer existed in the United States. By 1970 the United States was producing all out—at the rate of 10 million barrels a day. That was unfortunate from all points of view and should not be taken as a desirable standard to judge the performance of the oil industry, which if anything has tended to overproduce rather than underproduce.

In sum, the United States should basically rely on the market. The main function of the government is to make sure that irregularities to which the market is prone will not have damaging effects. The best way to do so is through a variable tariff with a low trigger price.

JOHN H. LICHTBLAU

Oil Import Dependency and Crises

I have recently attended several conferences on oil and national security. At each, including this one, the right questions have been asked, the correct data provided, and the appropriate analysis made. In short, the problem is clearly elaborated. Less clear is what can or should be done about it. Perhaps the problem of the national security consequences of rising U.S. oil imports is not subject to solution: we may have to learn to live with it.

Three, four, five years ago, when the price of oil was $27 to $28 a barrel, consensus projections were that U.S. oil consumption would rise, production would fall, and U.S. oil imports would steadily increase. Yet scarcely anyone thought before mid-1985 that the nominal price of oil could go to or below $20 a barrel for the rest of the 1980s. If those projections were at all realistic then, when the price of oil was $10 higher than it is today, they are all the more accurate now; the trend toward rising oil consumption, declining production, and increasing U.S. imports might properly be seen as irreversible, even at somewhat higher prices than the current $18 to $19 level.

The question then becomes not whether, but at what rate, U.S. dependence on foreign oil will increase. It may be important to try to slow that rate down. Indeed, some cogent arguments for doing so have been advanced by other contributors to this volume. But I doubt that it will be possible to arrest, let alone reverse, the rise in imports over the next eight or ten years. Hence I would argue that U.S. energy policy should be based on the premise that U.S. dependency on foreign oil will grow for the foreseeable future. The only question is how rapidly.

In assessing this trend, it is important to differentiate between long-term oil dependency and short-term energy crises brought on by foreign supply disruptions. The two are often confused or used interchangeably. Yet they are different and require different policy responses. Recently the Petroleum Industry Research Foundation held a conference called Are We Moving toward Another Energy Crisis? The question was meant to be real, not rhetorical. Several speakers and commentators answered with a qualified yes. That is, they argued that the United States is moving toward another energy crisis simply because it faces greater foreign oil dependency.

If a high degree of foreign oil dependency constituted a crisis, Japan and much of Western Europe would be in a state of permanent crisis. Japan is 99 percent dependent, and most European countries 80 to 90 percent dependent, on foreign oil. Nonetheless, in the past thirty years, these countries have faced energy crises only twice—no more often than the United States, which was producing, on both occasions, 10 million barrels a day, or well over half its oil requirements. The relation between the degree of oil import dependency and the probability of an energy crisis is not as obvious as it is sometimes made out to be.

An energy crisis is clearly a possibility, one that could happen at any time—or not happen at all. If the Strait of Hormuz is closed or Saudi Arabia's export facilities are destroyed or blocked, a world oil supply crisis will result in time. The United States would be deeply involved in that crisis, whether its import dependency were 25 percent or 50 percent. In either case, it would have to import its marginal requirements. With supply visibly tightening on world markets, domestic as well as foreign prices would soar. U.S. domestic prices would move right along unless the government were to impose controls.

During the 1973 and 1979 supply disruptions, the United States could do little to cope with the problem. Today it can use the strategic petroleum reserve (SPR) of nearly 540 million barrels and growing. Although I would like to see the reserve built up to the congressionally mandated level of 750 million barrels, it is already quite respectable. It can be drawn down by some 3 mmbd, nearly half of current U.S. oil import requirements. It is unlikely that a supply interruption in the Middle East would be so severe as to deprive the United States of that much of its imports. I am not counseling complacency. The SPR may not remain adequate if the level of U.S. oil imports keeps rising. But if a disruption should be of such proportions that it threatens to drain the U.S. reserve and similar emergency reserves in the other industrial countries, those countries would have to look outside the energy sector for appropriate remedies. Regarding the likelihood of such an event, one should keep in mind that a sustained oil disruption would be even more costly and more damaging to the disrupted suppliers than to their customers.

The magnitude of a disruption crisis is a function of the size of the global excess producing capacity. The U.S. oil import dependency ratio is a crucial factor in this equation because the increase in U.S. imports is likely to be the single most important element in the growth of OPEC oil exports and, hence, in the decline of its excess producing capacity.

To assess the future of the relation between OPEC exports and U.S. imports, some price assumptions are necessary. For this purpose, I assume that the present price of $18 to $19 a barrel continues, adjusted for inflation, through 1995. Although this price represents a significant recovery from the collapse of 1986, it would probably keep the *nominal* price below the 1985 level throughout the period. What effect would this price have on the demand for OPEC oil?

Through the first half of the 1980s OPEC exports kept declining despite a gradual price erosion from the 1981 peak. Only the 50 percent price crash in 1986 managed to reverse this trend, bringing about an increase of 2 mmbd in OPEC exports. The turnaround was costly for OPEC. To sell the additional 2 mmbd, OPEC lost 45 percent of its revenues, or $60 billion, over the course of the year. To make matters worse, part of the increase in export volume proved to be temporary. In 1987 OPEC exports will be only 1.5 mmbd above the 1985 level, despite continued comparatively low prices.

OPEC is not likely to find that 1988 will be any better. Worldwide changes in energy consumption and the rising availability of competitive fuels have weakened the demand response to lower oil prices. OPEC has therefore not regained its role as the world's marginal oil supplier. The present price is still sufficient to stimulate oil exploration and development in many geologically low-cost areas, mostly outside the United States. Exploration and development are also encouraged by cost reductions and by reductions in taxes, particularly in the United Kingdom, Canada, and Norway. Interestingly, the United States is an exception. It has not changed its fiscal regime to take cognizance of the price crash, maintaining its now anachronistic windfall profit tax.

If current real prices are maintained, oil requirements per unit of

GNP will continue to fall in the United States, as well as in other industrial countries. At the same time, other fuels will continue to substitute for oil, though more in Europe and Japan than in the United States, where natural gas prices may exceed fuel oil prices in some areas within a few years, reducing that form of substitution. Nuclear power will start leveling off in the United States in the next five years, but will continue to expand and substitute for fossil fuels in Japan and Western Europe at least until the end of the century. In transportation, however, oil use will grow. World consumption of gasoline may well be 1 to 1.5 mmbd higher in 1995 than it was in 1986.

Oil consumption in the developing countries, excluding OPEC, amounted to 9 mmbd in 1986, while production was 11 mmbd. Demand is likely to grow faster than production, providing a modestly rising market for OPEC exports, starting from a low base.

But the real key to how fast OPEC can increase its exports is the United States. Domestic oil consumption could rise about 1.5 mmbd between 1986 and 1995, a larger increase than is expected from Europe and Japan combined. A similar contribution to higher U.S. import requirements can be expected from the supply side. In 1988 production in the lower forty-eight states could well average about 1 mmbd below the 1985 level. Reductions in exploration costs will at best slow the decline, not stabilize production. In Alaska, oil production, now 1.9 mmbd, is likely to peak in 1989 and start falling after 1990.

By 1995 the decline in production and increase in demand could require an increase in net U.S. imports of at least 3 mmbd over the 1986 level of 5.4 mmbd. U.S. net oil import dependency would then be close to 50 percent, compared with 27 percent in 1985. Canadian light crude exports to the United States are likely to decline during this period and will not be fully replaced by increases in exports of heavy oil. Mexican oil exports to the United States may remain at approximately present levels. If so, the increase in oil imports from overseas will be greater than the total increase in U.S. oil imports. Directly, or indirectly, these imports will have to be supplied by the world's marginal supplier, that is, OPEC, and within OPEC, the Middle East.

To recapitulate, the most important element in the recovery of OPEC exports by the mid-1990s are U.S. oil import requirements along the lines I have outlined. Even then, OPEC will still have well over 20 percent of its producing capacity idle, but much more of this excess capacity will be concentrated in the Persian Gulf than it is today. The president and others have said the Gulf has substantial geopolitical and logistic significance for oil importers, particularly the United States. Presumably, the importance will be even greater by the mid-1990s.

If U.S. policymakers decide that the growing level of oil imports is a threat to national security, they may intervene in the market to stimulate domestic production and restrain consumption. If that strategy works, OPEC would have to bear the consequences. Whether OPEC would be able or willing to maintain existing prices in the absence of rising export demand is open to question. OPEC's current official sales price of $18 is still far above the marginal production cost of the highest-cost producer in the cartel. In this sense, there is much room to cut prices and set off recurrent volatility in the industry.

A stable oil price of roughly $20 to $21 in constant 1987 dollars for the next six to eight years would clearly be preferable from the points of view of OPEC, other oil exporters, and the United States and other high-cost producers. It would also alleviate the U.S. national security concern. As of now, however, the chances for such a producer-friendly global price stability are low. Whether we should or could obtain price stability for domestic producers will be a key issue in the new U.S. energy policy debate.

General Discussion

DiBona questioned the comparatively comforting outlook pictured by his fellow panel members. Evidence drawn from surveys of U.S. oil companies made by his association pointed the other way. These surveys suggested that U.S. oil production would decline sharply at prices in the neighborhood of $15 a barrel and would stabilize over the next several years only at prices in the range of $25 to $28 a barrel. As an example, in 1986 when prices and drilling fell off, new finds in the United States covered less than half of production. Furthermore, oil company geologists, who are congenital optimists on drilling prospects, see declining production for non-OPEC countries as a group at current prices. On the demand side, DiBona sees a pickup in the rest of the world but not so rapidly as in the United States. Finally, he sees little to justify the view that OPEC would be more sober minded in the future. Most of the time OPEC followed rather than set prices. It began to restrict production to fix prices only a few years ago. Thus at precisely the time when the public perceived OPEC to be coming apart, it was in fact behaving as a cartel for the first time.

Houthakker disagreed that non-OPEC production is destined to decline. There are still new discoveries that have not been exploited and that will come into production in the near future. Colombia, for example, is now becoming a sizable producer. Recently, the largest new discoveries since 1974 were announced in the North Sea, and much of the Norwegian sector is only now beginning to be explored. Hence there is reason to be optimistic about non-OPEC production outside the United States. Nor is Alaska facing a period of decline. Prudhoe Bay may well have peaked, but a number of small fields are still gearing up for higher production. The pipeline is likely to remain full at least until 1995. Furthermore, the biggest question mark of all in Alaska is the Arctic National Wildlife Refuge (ANWR), which may have as much as 25 billion barrels. If the engineers find ways of getting this oil out, the Alaska pipeline will continue to be filled for many years to come.

Lichtblau said the 1986 $15 price and the 1987 $18 price were probably too low to replace reserves and keep existing production.

Fred Singer supported an import fee as insurance against price collapse, but said it was important not to set the price so high that it becomes a subsidy to producers. He disagreed with Houthakker on the usefulness of maintaining excess production capacity, saying that the existing government-owned fields should be sold to the private sector because they had little to do with national security. He also thought that rising U.S. dependence on oil imports bore little relation to the large swings in the world price of oil. The two issues require different policies and should be distinguished from each other. Finally, he commented that if the reflagging of the Kuwaiti tankers brought lower oil prices, why not also reflag Iranian tankers or send in the U.S. Marines to bring the price of oil down to competitive levels.

Houthakker had no brief for the government's owning petroleum producing reserves, but as long as they existed, the government should not run the wells flat out. Going to the reflagging question, he said that U.S. and allied naval operations in the Gulf helped to keep sea-lanes open and enabled Iranian oil to keep flowing to markets. That brought benefits to all oil importers, including the United States.

Bruce Netschert thought the discussion indicated that increasing U.S. dependence on oil imports is not a cause for concern. Is that the right conclusion, he asked?

Lichtblau would not go that far. Rising U.S. oil dependency is a matter of concern but not a catastrophe. We will have to live with it. Even a high degree of dependency would not mean that five years from now OPEC will decide to increase the price of oil by 50 percent or 100 percent. That may never happen again because OPEC countries have learned about price elasticity and its consequences for oil markets. On the other hand, rising dependency on the Middle East is politically troubling. Other things equal, 25 percent dependency is preferable to 50 percent dependency. If there are ways of slowing down the rate of dependency and they are not too expensive or too arbitrary, we should use them. As a superpower, we do not want our freedom of action to be curtailed by dependence on oil from certain areas. Within the oil and energy sectors, however, high import dependency is no more significant to us than it has been for most other industrial countries that have lived with it for a long time.

Perspectives on the Energy Security Issue

WILLIAM B. QUANDT

The Middle East Factor

When talking about long-term energy predictions, analysts add the caveat that much depends on what happens in the Middle East. The lessons of the 1970s make such reminders only prudent.

The link between U.S. energy security and the Middle East derives from the extraordinary concentration of oil resources in the Persian Gulf area. In the first half of 1987 Saudi Arabia, Iran, Iraq, the Gulf Emirates, and Kuwait were producing about 10 million barrels a day, 40 percent of the oil moving in world trade and 20 percent of total oil consumption in noncommunist countries.

Even more remarkable is the concentration in this region of the world's spare production capacity. Saudi Arabia alone has some 4 to 5 mmbd. Iraq could probably increase production considerably. It has very large reserves, and current production is constrained primarily by limitations in transportation outlets. Kuwait has more than 1 mmbd of spare capacity, and the other Gulf states, including Iran, could together increase production at least 2 mmbd in relatively short order.

While the link between U.S. energy security and Middle East stability is obvious, its exact nature is less clear. We should look carefully at the experiences of the 1970s and the early 1980s before we speculate about potential threats to energy security arising in the Gulf.

In the 1970s the United States experienced two oil shocks. One was associated with the Arab-Israeli war of 1973 and the decision by most Arab oil producers to cut production and impose an embargo. The actual withdrawal of oil from the world market was probably some 2 to 3 mmbd. Within a few months production returned to the preembargo level. In 1978 and 1979 Iranian oil production declined precipitously, largely because of revolutionary turmoil, the departure of foreign workers, and strikes in the oil fields. The amount of oil removed from the market remained large for two to three months.

Then production began to recover, settling down after a while to about half the prerevolution level. In both cases, however, despite the recovery of production, prices shot up dramatically.

At the time it was easy to conclude that the disruptions inevitably brought on the big price run-ups. Yet we now understand better what really happened. The embargo itself did not cause the price to go up in 1973–74. In fact, the embargo was easily circumvented. What the embargo and the uncertainty created by the embargo did was to accelerate the upward pressure on prices that existed before 1973. Instead of rising gradually, oil prices jumped suddenly and sharply, only to level off and even to decline in real terms over the next few years.

During the brief period of supply uncertainties, consumers rushed to build stockpiles. With demand increasing abnormally at the very time that supplies were cut, prices increased sharply. The adjustment that normally would have followed was under way by the mid-1970s but was disrupted by the Iranian revolution, which again created vast uncertainty about future supplies. Nobody could know where the Iranian revolution was heading or whether Iranian production would return to customary levels.

As in 1973, uncertainty led to rapid stockpiling, this time from already low stocks. Little spare capacity existed anywhere in the world except in the Gulf. Once again, therefore, the price of oil rose sharply and abruptly. Prices then began to come down and would have done so more rapidly except that the Iran-Iraq war began in September 1980. In 1979 those countries together produced 6.8 mmbd; in 1981, only 2.4 mmbd. That disruption of oil supplies did not push prices back up, but it probably slowed the decline that had already begun.

If the experiences of the 1970s have somewhat exaggerated the link between Middle East instability and rising oil prices, the experiences of the 1980s show that Middle East instability and war can go hand in hand with declining oil prices. With Iran and Iraq at war, the price of oil fell from about $35 a barrel in 1981 to a low of $10 a barrel in 1986.

Other disturbances in the Middle East might also have created uncertainty in the oil market and put pressure on prices. The Mecca Mosque affair in 1979 and the Saudi riots in the eastern province in 1980 raised the specter of Saudi instability and a revolution on the Iranian model. In fact, however, the Saudi situation remained much more stable than most observers had expected.

The tanker war in the Gulf has been another source of market anxiety. But tankers have never stopped going into the Gulf, and oil has come out in undiminished supply. Furthermore, the tanker war has added to the incentives to build alternative transportation channels, principally pipelines to circumvent transit through the Gulf.

Since the outbreak of the Iran-Iraq war in 1980, both combatants have worked hard to increase oil production, primarily to finance the war. Iraq has more than doubled production from its low point in 1981. It exported about 2 mmbd in 1987 and now plans to boost shipments through pipelines in Turkey and Saudi Arabia that are about to be completed or are on the drawing board.

Iran has also managed to keep oil production at respectable levels— in the neighborhood of 2 mmbd most of the time despite Iraqi attempts to shut down Iran's production, storage, and transportation facilities. Iran also has plans for pipelines, though it is not clear whether they will be realized.

The coexistence during the 1980s of Middle East tension and ample oil supplies does not mean that there is no danger of oil supply instability from that area. Two supply disruption scenarios and a price collapse contingency deserve attention.

First, an Iranian victory over Iraq in the ground war would put Iran in a strong position to curtail Iraq's oil output and intimidate the Saudis into pursuing a restrictive oil production policy. In other words, Iran—usually the price hawk—would be in a position to push for higher prices within OPEC against relatively little resistance. Certainly the Saudis and Iraqis would find it difficult to use spare capacity to moderate prices.

A second possibility would be a major upheaval in Saudi Arabia along the lines of the revolution in Iran. The availability of the Saudi oil and the ability of Saudi Arabia to maintain spare capacity to keep prices stable would then be brought into sharp question.

A third development—truce in the Iran-Iraq war—could also be a source of instability. Iranian and Iraqi oil could flood the market as both countries seek to expand market share, increase revenues rapidly, and try to rebuild their economies or their armies for the next round of war. Low prices over a sustained period could then set the stage for a tightening market in the future and a heightened security vulnerability to a supply interruption.

The two disruption scenarios are possible, but not likely. For the next few years at least, I do not see an oil shock coming out of the

Iran-Iraq war or out of an upheaval in Saudi Arabia. The most likely development is that sometime in the next several years the Iran-Iraq war will come to an end. It is never wise to predict when, but an end will come. It could take the form of a truce or a cease-fire, and we may be closer to that moment than many people realize. If that happens, prices will be under considerable downward pressure.

Some think that sustained downward price pressure is a threat to energy security in the sense that it stimulates oil consumption and discourages oil exploration, making the market more vulnerable to a subsequent price jump. I would much rather confront that kind of a threat than the threat of oil disruptions with much higher prices. There are public policy steps that could be taken to guard against the uncertainties caused by lower prices. On balance, low prices are an economic plus, though the potential volatility of prices is a concern that should be confronted.

This relatively relaxed picture of Middle East oil supplies—now conventional wisdom—depends heavily on the availability of considerable spare capacity in a few countries, particularly Saudi Arabia, and on rather flat trends in world oil consumption. If consumption rises steadily, exploration outside of OPEC goes down, and spare capacity outside the Gulf disappears, it is evident that sometime in the 1990s Saudi Arabia, Iran, and Iraq are going to have a huge influence over the price of oil. In those circumstances the market could be vulnerable even to relatively small oil supply disruptions, much less large Gulf disruptions.

To expect the Middle East to become a pleasant, peaceful, stable region is the height of wishful thinking. There is every reason to expect considerable turmoil, hostilities, and perhaps renewed warfare. Then the events of the 1970s might be a considerably better model for what might happen sometime in the 1990s. The question is whether the United States needs to take actions now to be better prepared in the 1990s for possible disruptions that might be coming our way.

HENRY S. ROWEN

U.S. Vulnerability to an Interruption in Gulf Oil Supplies

The ongoing conflict in the Persian Gulf provides daily reminders that the world's largest low-cost source of energy is also in one of the world's politically least stable areas. Moreover, it lies uncomfortably close to the Soviet Union and to Soviet military power, elements of which are present in Afghanistan, the Arabian peninsula, South Yemen, and Ethiopia. The conjunction of these two factors is troublesome, yet often ignored.

I am going to cite six frequently stated reasons why we should not worry very much about the security of the supply of oil from the Persian Gulf and then explain why I consider them to be unsatisfactory.

The most familiar American arguments are:

—The market will solve the problem, if there is a problem.

—The oil exporters need the money and therefore will have to sell the oil, no matter who gets control of the country concerned.

—Oil security is a problem for the Europeans and Japanese, not for Americans.

—A Soviet move to control this oil would mean World War III; therefore, the USSR will not try to take over the Persian Gulf oil countries.

Characteristic views in Europe and Japan are:

—Oil security is an American, not a European or Japanese, problem.

—The main source of instability is the Arab-Israeli conflict. If Israel would come to an agreement with the Palestinian Liberation Organization, the problem would go away. This argument was popular a few years ago but not so much now. It will reemerge.

These propositions are either false, or only partly true, or mutually contradictory, as in the counterclaims about the locus of the oil security problem.

FIGURE 1. *Potential Economic Costs to the United States from the Loss of One-Half of Persian Gulf Oil Supplies for One Year, 1965–2000*

Percent loss of U.S. GNP

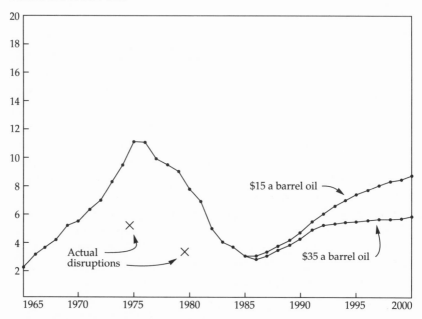

Consider first the observation that there is no oil security problem, or at least not one for the United States. Figure 1 shows an index of costs to the U.S. economy from a major oil disruption, defined as the loss of one-half of Persian Gulf oil supplies for one year. That is a large but not a farfetched disruption. This figure also shows the estimated GNP loss in the United States from the oil supply disruptions that actually occurred in 1973 and 1979–80. In 1973–74 the loss in U.S. output is estimated at 5 percent and in 1979–80 at 3 percent. We survived but did not enjoy the experience. These actual cases refute the proposition that producers have to supply the oil; they did not and we suffered. Calculations for Western Europe and Japan would show similar results, reflecting the close links among the U.S., European, and Japanese economies.

These were substantial losses. It can be argued that they were large because of the high degree of world market dependence on Persian Gulf oil existing on those occasions. In fact, the West's dependence on Persian Gulf oil has varied considerably in the past two decades. The left-hand half of figure 1 shows how U.S. exposure to disruptions in the Gulf changed in this period. It grew remarkably from the mid-1960s to the mid-1970s and then fell equally remarkably through the mid-1980s. There are two reasons for this wide swing. The first is the Persian Gulf share of noncommunist world oil production. In 1965 it was about 31 percent, reached a peak of 44 percent in 1975, and then fell back to 31 percent by 1985. The second factor is the degree of U.S. oil import dependency. The share of U.S. oil imports in oil consumption went from 18 percent in 1965 to a peak of 38 percent in 1975–80, declining to 31 percent in 1985.

In short, the noncommunist world became more dependent and then less dependent on Persian Gulf oil, and the United States became more dependent and then less dependent on oil imports. Those changes were driven mainly by changes in the price of oil. Generally, when dependence was large, potential losses were large. They declined when dependence on these two factors declined.

As a rule of thumb, roughly two-thirds of the U.S. loss from a large oil supply disruption comes from the dependence of the world on Persian Gulf oil and one-third from the U.S. dependence on oil imports. This means that even if the United States imported no oil, it would experience about two-thirds of the GNP loss shown in figure 1 because of the worldwide economic dislocation caused by the sharp run-up in the price. Market forces are not a universal solution; they made matters worse in the late 1960s and early 1970s and they made them better in the past decade.

So much for the past. We are now witnessing a reversal of the favorable trend of the last decade. In terms of Persian Gulf dependence and the exposure to economic losses, the balance of this century is shaping up as a replay, not of the 1970s, but of the late 1960s and the first half of the 1970s. We are experiencing a growing vulnerability to a Persian Gulf oil disruption.

This vulnerability is shown in the right half of figure 1. Very much depends on the price of oil from now to the end of the century. That price will in fact fluctuate a great deal. For present purposes, however, I assume it will remain the same throughout the period—either at $15 a barrel or at $35 a barrel in constant 1985 dollars. At $15 a barrel oil consumption would be higher and therefore exposure to potential losses from a supply disruption would be larger. At a price of $35 a barrel, oil consumption would be smaller as would exposure to disruption losses. This relation is reflected in the exposure to potential loss projections for each price, as shown in figure 1.

The results indicate that exposure to disruptive losses will grow, though even for the low price it will not reach the peak shown for the mid-1970s. Since then, there have been major structural changes in the use of oil, which are slow to reverse. For the next few years the loss exposure stays relatively low because of excess supply capacity outside the Gulf. Excess capacity is used up by 1990–92, and potential losses then start to climb.

These calculations of potential losses are subject to a great deal of uncertainty. For example, they change significantly under different assumptions about price elasticities. Furthermore, they do not take into account the effect of using the strategic petroleum reserve in an emergency, which would reduce possible losses.

Nonetheless, these projections show that the loss of one-half of Persian Gulf oil for a year would have substantial adverse economic effects. That is a problem the market will not solve; if anything, the market is now making the problem worse.

I turn now to the argument that the Arab-Israeli conflict is the root cause of the oil security problem. In the first place, that argument is hard to square with what is now going on in the Gulf. Nor does it help much to explain the first oil price shock. With the benefit of hindsight, it is evident that the price of oil was going to increase sharply in the early 1970s. It might not have gone up as sharply as it did if the Arab-Israeli war in 1973 had not occurred. The sharpness of that price increase did a lot of damage. But what is most obvious about the Gulf region is that the Arab-Israeli relationship is not the only source of instability.

What about the proposition that there is nothing to worry about from the Soviet Union because a Soviet military move to take over part or all of the Persian Gulf region would mean World War III? Indeed, President Carter in his 1980 State of the Union address said: "Any attempt by an outside force to gain control of the Persian Gulf region will be regarded as an assault on the vital interests of the United States of America. Any such assault will be repelled by the use of any means necessary, including military force."

This statement leaves little room for ambiguity. Whether the United States has the means to repel such an assault, however, is open to question. The Persian Gulf is very far from the United States and very close to the Soviet Union. The fact that the countries in the area are reluctant to have an American military presence within their borders—even today when we are involved in naval operations in the Gulf that they welcome—indicates additional problems for us in trying to protect oil interests. Western European countries and Japan show a similar reluctance to take action to protect access to oil supplies. Their interest in containing Soviet influence and keeping free access to the oil resources of the Gulf is at least as strong as that of the United States, but it has been hard to get them to help. Their participation in the Persian Gulf naval operation is a new and welcome change. By and large, however, protecting the Gulf is seen as an American responsibility. Yet joint Western European and Japanese participation is necessary for political as well as military reasons.

Serious instability is always a threat to the region. William Quandt mentioned some possibilities. There are others; for example, internal destabilization and perhaps conflict within Iran. Some such development could lead to an increase in Soviet influence and possible disturbance to the oil supply chain. Over the longer-term, moreover, the potential for Soviet military moves in the region should be a cause for continuing concern.

What might be done to contain these dangers? Earlier in the game—the mid-1970s—the answer was U.S. energy independence. That approach is essentially wrong, but not entirely foolish. As I indicated earlier, about one-third of our losses in these disruptions comes from dependence on oil imports.

Hendrik Houthakker mentioned that a tariff on oil might have been useful at one time. William Hogan, in a recent report, argues for a tariff on oil now as a measure to reduce U.S. exposure to politically caused supply disruptions.[1] Another possible action is a domestic tax on all oil, especially gasoline. These actions, along with building up the strategic petroleum reserve, would be part of our oil security strategy.

Another component of that strategy should be political-military.

---

1. William W. Hogan and Bijan Mossavar-Rahmani, *Energy Security Revisited* (Harvard University, Energy and Environmental Policy Center, 1987).

It should seek to maintain access to the region through concerted action with Western European countries and Japan.

In sum, U.S. oil security strategy should be twofold: (1) maintaining military presence and power to deter and to limit the worse disruption possibilities, and (2) reducing our exposure to economic damage if the worst occurs.

Oil Security: An Economic Phenomenon

Few important concepts have turned out to be as slippery to define as oil security. That is surprising when one considers the effort devoted to its analysis since the oil embargo and price shock of 1973–74 made the subject a world-class worry. It has raised political, military, economic, financial, and commercial concerns, most of which, with the benefit of hindsight and a costly learning experience, proved to be overblown or wrongheaded. My thesis, which I share with Harry Rowen, is that the core of the energy security problem is to avoid or mitigate the cost of price shocks in the event of an interruption of oil supplies. That is a serious but not an unmanageable problem.

WHY SO MUCH ATTENTION TO OIL?

Oil and energy's size and volatility in the world economy is a good place to begin. It makes sense, for this purpose, to couple oil with other energy fuels because changes in the supply and price of oil, with a lag, affect the price and supply of other fuels.

At today's prices, the value of primary energy production amounts to about 4½ percent of world economic output, with oil accounting for almost half. That makes energy production worth three times the value of all food grain production (rice, wheat, and coarse grains). A similar story applies to trade. Oil exports alone account for about 6 percent of total world exports and are almost five times as large as the value of all food grain exports.

Oil's economic volatility is even more important. In 1970, when oil was still comparatively cheap and consumption growing rapidly, primary energy output was equal to 1.7 percent of world GNP and oil less than 1.0 percent. In 1981, when the price of oil reached its peak, energy production constituted 10 percent, and oil 6 percent, of world output. Swings of this magnitude in the space of a decade necessarily set in motion vast structural economic changes throughout the world.

Concern about security of supply is the third element making oil different if not unique. Various aspects of this concern have already been discussed. Sixty percent of the world's oil reserves and three-fourths of present excess productive capacity are located in the Persian Gulf region. Supply interruptions have occurred there in the past and, in view of the political instability in the area, are likely to recur in the future. Tension in the Gulf from the Iran-Iraq war, now in its eighth year, underlines the point.

LESSONS FROM THE PAST

These characteristics of the industry explain why security of oil supply is so sensitive an issue for oil importers. They also account for the severe reactions to the oil embargo and price jumps of 1973–1974 and their aftermath.

It is useful to recall that concern about energy security, mainly confined to the United States, long preceded 1973. In 1958 the United States established oil import quotas on national security grounds even though the world industry was in oversupply. These quotas lasted almost fifteen years, serving to slow down the decline of the U.S. oil industry at the cost of using up our high-cost reserves while forgoing the use of low-cost Middle East reserves. Americans, therefore, paid about 50 percent more for oil than the world price. Also during this period, anxiety arose about the emergence of the Soviet Union as an oil exporter on the argument that the so-called Soviet oil offensive could ultimately create political mischief. This issue eventually faded away only to reemerge some fifteen years later in security worries about undue dependence of Western Europe on imports of Soviet natural gas.

Energy security became a serious matter for all oil importers only after the traumatic events of 1973–74. These events forced consumers everywhere to address an area that had been taken for granted. Oil, after all, had been driving out other primary energy fuels because it was cheap, plentiful, and reliable. In this new situation, it was necessary to build up information to understand why such fundamental changes were happening and to judge whether they would continue. In an atmosphere of near panic, the sensible arguments and actions had to be distinguished from the not so sensible. All this took time.

Political reactions among the industrial countries—amounting at times almost to a beggar-thy-neighbor oil policy—were a prime example of this process. They ran a troubled course until common sense took hold. Even so, political rationality in the face of oil supply interruptions is not to be taken for granted.

Since oil is a fungible commodity, the selective embargo against the United States and the Netherlands in 1973 proved to have little effect on the distribution of oil among importing countries. The major oil companies managed the problem equitably and effectively. Nonetheless, some countries sought to assure themselves of favored access to supply through bilateral deals that proved to be a wasted effort. They provided only the opportunity to buy oil at prevailing world prices—sometimes even at a premium—which was hardly an advantage. It took time for the realization to sink in that price was what mattered and that whatever oil was available would be allocated on the basis of price. Damaging important military and political alliances to achieve imaginary oil supply assurances made no sense. This unseemly scramble for supply security eventually petered out, but it was not a distinguished performance.

A similar point applies to the often-made argument that oil importing countries with few domestic energy resources, such as Japan, are more vulnerable to an oil supply interruption than more fortunately endowed countries such as the the United States. That would be true in a general war situation in which supply lines could be interrupted over a protracted period. In the usual case, however, logic and experience run against that argument. To be sure, countries that have little or no oil incur larger terms-of-trade losses when prices go up. Beyond that, reductions in oil supply have been roughly proportionate among oil importing countries, and each has had to cope with similar economic disruption problems from the jump in oil prices. Some with little or no oil fared better than the average, simply because their economic adjustment policies were more efficient.

What can be said generally about the military factor in energy security? Consumption of oil for military purposes is comparatively small. In the United States, peacetime use for the military accounts for little more than 2 percent of total oil consumption—too small to be affected by temporary supply interruptions. In a conventional full-scale war, U.S. military requirements might triple. They would receive top priority, leaving the burden of restraint to fall on the civilian sector. The effect on countries with few energy resources would depend on the state of supply lines, but in all likelihood losses on this account would be severe.

That said, the military factor in energy security, while causing unease, is generally murky and linkages are far from clear. A general war, whose dimension and duration are largely unpredictable, amounts to a contingency whose consequences would overwhelm problems arising from threats to the supply of oil. On these grounds alone, I am among the skeptics Harry Rowen cites who do not believe the USSR would risk going to war with the United States over oil.

How then should one view the concentration of naval forces from the United States and other Western countries in the Persian Gulf? Does it suggest a close link between military and energy security? Surely, however, there is no oil supply problem at the present time. Rather, I think it fair to say that the United States and other Western countries strongly wish to see the Iran-Iraq war end, and at the least to discourage its intensification. They also want to avoid an Iranian victory, which could be a threat to moderate governments in the region and possibly to stable oil supplies in the future.

Fears about the financial consequences also drew wide attention in the early aftermath of the first oil shock. The arguments proved to be entirely farfetched. In the first two years or so, oil exporters rapidly accumulated foreign exchange because their capacity or willingness to increase their consumption of imported goods and services ran behind the increase in their oil receipts. Extrapolations of these early results produced vastly overblown projections of the future size of their financial accumulations. Some argued that the capital surplus oil exporters would shift their holdings from one currency to another, either to exert political pressure on the United States and its allies or to maximize financial returns. In either event, this "sloshing around of oil money" on so vast a scale would keep exchange rates in turmoil and ultimately cause the international financial system to collapse. It was also argued, sometimes alternatively, sometimes not, that these financial accumulations would enable oil exporters "to buy up the world" through vast foreign equity investments, with political consequences of no small proportions.

Like some other aspects of the energy security discussion, these financial fears heavily discounted the inherent flexibility of the economic system. Oversimplified extrapolation of early trends left no room for economic forces to do their work—for example, in dampening energy consumption, encouraging worldwide oil exploration and interfuel substitution, and in causing large increases in asset prices in reponse to a sudden escalation of demand. Furthermore, the strong, continuing push toward the internationalization of capital markets hardly entered the analysis. Today's movement of capital around the world dwarfs the accumulation of oil money fifteen years ago. Furthermore, the fears of that time failed to recognize that holders of capital—whether from oil or anything else—require a strong international system to maximize earnings while maintaining liquidity. In short, their interests converge with the general interest.

THE ECONOMIC DIMENSION

That brings me to my main point, namely, that energy security for oil importers is an economic problem—developing the capacity to reduce the economic losses from a sudden price jump, such as could arise from a serious oil supply interruption.

Price shocks come about from shortages of other commodities, but they do not pose the same danger. Consider for example the tripling of grain prices and the explosion of industrial materials prices in 1972–73. The quantitative significance of the boom in these other commodities was much smaller and the readjustment took place much sooner than was true for oil. As a result, the nonoil commodity price shocks and the consequent economic disruption losses were much smaller in scale.

In essence, disruption losses arise because modern economies are not flexible enough to adjust smoothly to very large external shocks, such as a sudden jump in the price of oil. Other prices do not fall when oil prices rise and wages tend to be rigid as labor seeks to avoid the real income losses from rising energy costs. Inflationary pressures then mount. The sudden large distortions in international payment balances tend to constrain trade and monetary policies. All this creates widespread uncertainty, which then dampens investment and consumption. The feedback effect of similar developments in other oil importing countries adds to the cumulation of downside economic pressures.

These economic losses are not easy to quantify, but available estimates indicate they have been very large. Calculations by the OECD and others suggest that the 1979–80 oil price shock caused world production by 1982 to be about 6 percent lower than it otherwise would have been, amounting to a cumulative loss in output over the period of about $1 trillion. That loss, it should be emphasized, is independent of the importers' loss in income from the deterioration in their terms of trade. Initially, the 1979–80 oil price jump transferred about $150 billion from oil importers to oil exporters, an amount that diminished in subsequent years as the volume of oil consumption declined and the price fell. Unlike these terms-of-trade income transfers, the large economic disruption losses of output in oil importing countries had no counterpart gains for oil exporters. To the contrary, the reduction in economic output of oil importers and the accelerated replacement of oil-intensive equipment reduced the medium- and long-term demand for oil, causing steady downward pressure on its price and eventual economic costs to oil exporters as well.

Defining energy security principally in these terms leaves out some other economic issues that often are included. One is the battle over economic rents. These economic rents arise because the oil market is not competitive on the supply side. By restricting supply to maintain or increase these rents, exporters tend to overshoot underlying supply-demand realities, thereby creating market problems for themselves in the future. For their part, importers may seek to reduce these rents by imposing taxes on oil imports or subsidizing alternative fuels, advantageously or not. This more or less continuing struggle over economic rents between importers and exporters is distinct from the economic disruption costs arising from a supply interruption.

Similarly, energy security is also distinct from a rise in oil prices caused by growing resource scarcity. Depletion of oil resources and increasing costs of producing energy resources will usually lead to rising oil prices and lower real national income unless offset by technological advance. This loss cannot be avoided by either domestic or international energy policy. That is true whether the loss takes the form of an increase in the transfer of resources to foreign producers, or an increase in the cost of production of domestic energy resources, or the costs of switching to less energy-intensive methods of production or forms of consumption.

FUTURE SHOCKS?

Should an oil supply interruption occur in the future, would the economic disruption costs, proportionately, be much the same as in the past? Or would the learning experience of the past fifteen years and the reduced role of oil in the economy make a difference?

To address this question, I will use for my baseline a more or less conventional, surprise-free forecast of the world oil market over the next decade or so. Assume that world economic output will grow by almost 3 percent a year and oil consumption by 1 percent a year. Assume also that the real price of oil in the next ten years will rise gradually to $23 to $25 a barrel and the demand for OPEC crude will increase to 23–25 mmbd. That would also imply U.S. oil imports of 8 to 10 mmbd—sharply higher than the 6 mmbd we import now but not much more than peak U.S. imports of 8 mmbd in 1977. By the accepted rules of energy forecasting, these figures will be off by a considerable margin. Nonetheless, they point to the likelihood that sharply reduced but still substantial excess capacity will exist a decade from now, including a small amount outside the Persian Gulf.

If this market outlook is anywhere near right, the first point to make is that repetition of the two oil price shocks of the 1970s should not be expected, even by the mid-1990s. In each of those cases, a relatively small supply interruption—approximately 3 mmbd—touched off panic scrambles to increase stocks, which in turn led to rapid price escalation. In the oil environment I have projected, a supply interruption of that size should cause oil prices to rise only moderately, and then only because of uncertainty about whether supply problems would escalate. In the main, the likelihood of additional supply from trouble-free countries and the possible use of emergency stocks by importing countries should dampen market reactions. This fairly sanguine conclusion, moreover, does not allow for the probability that the reserve-rich OPEC countries, this time around, will wish to avoid another rapid run-up in oil prices and the adverse energy and oil market consequences they would see as likely to follow.

Closure of the Strait of Hormuz for a sustained period would be a different matter. In that extreme and unlikely contingency the market would in the first instance lose 7 to 8 mmbd, or 15 percent of world consumption. With no offsetting action prices could double or more, depending on perceptions about how long the emergency would last. Economic disruption costs might then approach the scale of those experienced after the price jumps of 1979–80.

In fact, so severe a market reaction even in this extreme situation is unlikely to recur. Offsetting measures would reduce the oil supply shortfall and moderate the run-up of prices and its economic consequences. Oil producing countries outside the Gulf would probably be able and willing to increase production and even in the mid–1990s should have 1 to 2 mmbd of excess capacity. Stocks stored elsewhere by Gulf countries could also be drawn down.

Most important, by the mid–1990s the realistically usable emergency stockpiles of the importing countries would have reached 1¼ billion barrels. There would be heated discussion in the International Energy Agency (IEA) about whether these stocks should be held back until it became clear that the interruption was temporary or that it would not become even more severe. In the end, however, sanity would prevail. Agreement would be reached on a coordinated drawdown of perhaps 4 mmbd to be sustained for at least six months if necessary. (That would still leave 40 percent of emergency reserves available for future use if the supply crisis persisted.)

All in all, these actions should offset as much as two-thirds of even so severe a supply interruption. Prices would rise substantially, possibly by one-third, which could still mean losses of about 2 percent of world GNP. Nonetheless, most of the potential economic disruption costs would have been avoided.

Despite rising U.S. oil imports, the fact remains that present rises in energy security, or those that are likely to exist ten years from now, compare favorably with the situations in 1973–74 and 1979–80, when production capacity was pushed to its limits, emergency stocks were low, and the policies of importing countries were in disarray.

POLICY IMPLICATIONS

Several policy conclusions follow from this assessment.

First, energy security, as I have sought to define it, can be examined only in relation to the world oil market, not to the U.S. oil position alone. As John Lichtblau and others have pointed out, the United States will be substantially dependent on oil imports no matter what actions it might reasonably take. Even with oil self-sufficiency, however, the United States would still suffer severe economic damage if a supply disruption caused another oil price shock on world markets. In ten years U.S. oil imports might amount to about one-third of total world imports. Whether this import dependency is dangerous will depend on the state of the world oil market at that time, not on the size of these imports as such.

Second, it follows that U.S. actions in energy should be coordinated to the maximum feasible degree with those of other industrial countries. Whatever we do to conserve oil or build emergency stocks will be made three times as effective in influencing the world market if other countries take comparable action. Obversely, if we fail to get such cooperation, the benefits of our actions on the U.S. economy could be diluted by a factor of three.

Third, the uncertainties applying to forecasts of the oil market ten years from now are very large. On the supply side, it is well to note that the production of non-OPEC countries was expected to peak some years ago, but it continues to increase. The Soviet Union at one time was projected to become a net importer by 1985, but its oil exports continue to grow. Although Soviet production may soon peak, possible gains from improved efficiency in oil use and from oil substitution are huge if the country ever gets its prices right. On the demand side, the question marks are also large, principally because the world use of oil moves steadily toward concentration on transportation fuels. The easy gains in efficiency have long since been realized. In the future, surprises may be on the disappointing side.

These uncertainties highlight the need to subject possible actions to careful cost-benefit tests. My own list is short. The United States should increase the rate of adding to the strategic petroleum reserve and persuade other countries to build or increase their government-held oil reserves as well. We can best do that by convincing them that U.S. stocks will be used to the full in an emergency in accordance with IEA agreements if other countries join now in adding to their stocks. No other action provides as effective a defense against oil price shocks and against the political use of oil.

Domestically, I agree with those who would eliminate the windfall profit tax. It is an anachronism and a needless disincentive to investment. A variable oil import fee to protect the industry against a sudden price collapse makes sense to me at the present time. I would set the trigger point at a minimum of $12 and no higher than $15 a barrel. Finally, the current market provides an excellent opportunity to complete the deregulation of natural gas, adding flexibility to the energy system at little or no immediate cost to the economy. I would also advocate a gasoline tax, but more on fiscal than on energy grounds. Whether more is needed should depend on how the world market outlook changes.

General Discussion

Quandt said the possibility of growing Soviet influence in Iran as raised by Rowen needed qualification. Despite the disruption of revolution and war, the Iranian system, far from disintegrating into factions, has proved to be remarkably durable. Soviet influence could indeed increase, not through Soviet military intervention, but from political and diplomatic effects related to the war with Iraq and the U.S. role in the Gulf. After the disaster of the Iran affair in 1986, the United States has conducted its military activities in the Gulf with a reasonable mixture of strength and restraint. Should we get into a serious military encounter, including attacking major military targets and politically important symbols inside Iran, we might create conditions under which Soviet influence would indeed grow. The Iranians do not wish to become dependent on the Soviet Union. If they find themselves in a state of war with the United States, however, they will turn to the Soviet Union for weapons and diplomatic support.

Quandt said it is not in the U.S. interest to treat Iran as a country with which we have a long-term adversary relationship. For the moment it is in our interest to ensure that Iran does not win the war. Tilting in Iraq's direction by our naval presence is appropriate. But that does not mean we should be looking for a big military confrontation with Iran.

Over the long term, Quandt said, we do not want Iran to slip into the Soviet orbit. Any glimmer of rationality in what the Reagan administration thought it was doing in the Iran-contra affair consisted of the recognition that Iran is an important country which we should not write off and to which lines should be open. That notion became confused with hostages and arms sales, but the point is still important. Although the United States is well positioned militarily in the Gulf, it should avoid an all-out confrontation with Iran. That would give the Soviets not so much a military but a political and diplomatic opening they would like to have.

Lichtblau asked what would have happened if the United States had not reflagged the Kuwaiti tankers. Would the Middle East oil supply have been unaffected? Was this policy wise?

Quandt replied that the U.S. action had had little effect on the supply of oil. The tanker war has gone on with virtually no change. There was a brief forty-five day period of comparative calm, but that was about it. On the other hand, the American military presence set the stage for intensifying the political debate within Iran over the wisdom of the war. Iran does not want to see the war with Iraq internationalized. The military presence of the United States and its Western allies helped make it respectable for a body of opinion inside Iran to argue that the war is not serving Iran's long-term interests, that Iran is getting isolated. Furthermore, the U.S. military presence put us in a strong position to go to the Soviets and talk about a strategy in the United Nations to end the war. It has been a long time since the United States and the USSR have agreed on a U.N. resolution calling for a cease-fire in a regional conflict. That agreement has something to do with the fact that the Soviets do not want to see us institutionalize our military presence in the Gulf—to gain bases in Saudi Arabia and Kuwait. This agreement could all come unstuck and our presence is a risky business. Nonetheless, we went into the Gulf, he thought, not to protect shipping but to affect the Iran-Iraq war on the ground.

Mary Beth Zimmerman asked each panelist whether in terms of public policy on energy security it was more important to reduce imports or build reserves and what was the best indicator of whether the policy was working.

Rowen answered that the single most important policy instrument is the strategic petroleum reserve.

Fried agreed and added that the best index of where we are is the state of the world oil market.

Quandt's indicator also was the state of the world oil market, as measured by the price of oil and the amount of excess capacity and where it exists.

Singer said he had difficulty in understanding the GNP loss from an oil shock. There are at least three different measures of the loss. One is the higher cost of importing oil. Another is the chance of shock, which causes dislocation in our production capacity. A third is the lack of fuel for transportation and factories, which causes unemployment. In the past, the procedure used to distribute oil, that is, allocations, caused the disruption. Much of the loss was due to our macroeconomic policy reactions to these price rises. If so, one should take into account how to respond to oil shocks in the future so that losses would not be as large as they were in the past.

Rowen said losses result from a combination of factors. First, oil importers suffer a terms-of-trade loss when prices go up. There is also a loss of output when the price goes up sharply. That causes dislocation and creates unemployment. These losses can be made worse by controls. We could take a bad situation and make it worse by creating further dislocations through controls. On the other hand, it is also possible to use policy instruments to reduce unemployment effects—for example, by increasing the money supply to mitigate the immediate demand-depressing effects of the shock, but this can add to inflationary pressure later on.

Michael Koleda said we did not do enough in the past to provide energy security and we are not doing enough now to give us greater flexibility and more options ten years from now should something go wrong under one or other of the scenarios that have been mentioned.

Quandt said we have done some useful things and should do more of the same now. A strategic petroleum reserve exists, and a number of controls that had a distorting effect have been eliminated. That is all to the good. The strategic petroleum reserve should be larger. The president, five or ten years from now, will have it to use in an emergency. We have a military capability for Gulf contingencies that is much better than it was ten or fifteen years ago. As a result, the president, a decade from now, will have more choices available than the president did ten years ago in the event of a sizable disruption in the Gulf.

An Official View

WILLIAM F. MARTIN

Energy Policy and U.S. National Priorities

When energy took on crisis proportions in the 1970s, governments probably responded too quickly and, therefore, sometimes foolishly. Crash programs tend to crash. Today in the midst of slack oil prices and a large worldwide surplus in oil production capacity, energy policy has to meet sterner tests. The period of calm is useful because energy security challenges lie ahead, and government must be prepared to know whether and how to respond. Critics sometimes claim the administration does not have an energy policy. I hope to dispel that notion here. In doing so, I want to emphasize that energy decisions must be seen in terms of how they affect the budget, the economy, national defense, and foreign policy. Energy is no longer an overriding issue taking precedence over other national priorities.

In the economic summit of 1980, the last one in which energy was the key issue, the heads of government predicted that the share of oil in total OECD energy demand would decline from 53 percent in 1980 to about 40 percent in 1990. Some of the changes they envisaged were not fulfilled and some were more than fulfilled, but the decline in oil's relative importance has been steady and sure; by 1987 oil's share in OECD primary energy had fallen to 43 percent.

A number of impressive developments in the 1980s were responsible. Coal consumption increased 35 percent, and nuclear power expanded sixfold, accounting now for 6 percent of total energy. Energy is used with increasing efficiency; despite OECD economic growth of 30 percent since 1973, energy consumption is no higher today than it was then. Also contributing to the decline in OPEC's influence over the market has been an increase of 25 percent in oil production from non-OPEC countries.

Nineteen eighty-six, however, was a troublesome year for the energy industry. Because of the oil price collapse, the U.S. industry lost almost 1 million barrels a day of production. The Chernobyl accident in the Soviet Union raised new questions about nuclear power everywhere. Attention focused on the acid rain issue and the consequences for coal use. And the Persian Gulf situation heated up. It was a good time to look in detail at the energy situation in the United States and to ask what if anything needed to be done about it. President Reagan asked Secretary of Energy John Herrington to address these issues. Our energy security study seeks to provide some answers.[1]

That study shows that U.S. oil imports are on the rise. The United States could be dependent on imported oil for 50 percent of its oil consumption in 1990 and for 60 percent in 1995. Oil imports in 1995 are estimated to be 8–10 mmbd, assuming that economic growth averages a moderate 2.4 percent a year and domestic oil production declines slowly.

Defining the problem is fairly straightforward. Solutions are harder to come by. Several basic principles guided our search.

A policy to reduce dependency on oil from the Persian Gulf, which is the basic energy security concern, should not focus on oil alone or the United States alone. Other energy sources must be considered, as must energy production and consumption in Western Europe, Japan, and the developing countries.

Another guiding principle, as I indicated earlier, is that energy security proposals be weighed against other administration policy goals. In short, what are the environmental, budgetary, national security, and macroeconomic effects?

We were strongly driven in our study by faith in the free market. I believe there is a broad consensus today that the free market approach to energy policy is the most efficient and workable.

At the same time, we recognize that the international market is not freely competitive on the supply side. Undue dependence of that market on a single source or on a coordinated group of suppliers increases vulnerability to price increases that can jeopardize both the world economy and U.S. national security. National security and energy security are linked.

I turn now to some of our recommendations and their current

1. U.S. Department of Energy, *Energy Security*, A Report to the President of the United States (Washington, D. C., 1987).

status. We made progress on a few; others are still awaiting congressional action.

We sought an increase in the strategic petroleum reserve (SPR). There are now 535 million barrels in the SPR; our goal is 750 million barrels. We are also urging allies to increase their emergency oil reserves. And we have had some success. Today strategic stocks in the industrialized countries could be released at a rate of 4 to 5 mmbd in the event of a severe oil disruption.

We opposed an oil import fee. The cost to the economy is too high for the incremental energy security. Initially, tax incentives for the domestic oil industry looked attractive; energy security benefits would be significant, and macroeconomic risks would be small. In the end, such proposals were rejected as being inconsistent with the 1986 Tax Reform Act. We recommended steps to open the Arctic National Wildlife Refuge to exploration, where reserves could be as large as those in Prudhoe Bay. Congress is now focusing its attention on that question.

We recommended development of clean coal technology. We asked Congress for $2.5 billion over the next five years to develop technologies to burn coal more cleanly. Developing such technologies would be more cost-effective than putting more stringent emission standards on power plants.

We proposed legislation to streamline licensing of nuclear power plants and at the same time improve the economies and supply of nuclear power.

Our study also recommended another look at alternative fuels such as ethanol and methanol. Because oil is crucial to energy security and because oil is primarily used for transportation, these alternative fuels could prove valuable. They could also help cities to meet environmental standards. We will report our findings on the economics and technology of these fuels in 1988.

The Reagan administration has also been active internationally in making energy supplies more secure. When the tanker war began in 1983, the United States had 250 million barrels in the SPR. Our strategy was to keep the Strait of Hormuz open, draw down stocks early in a crisis, and encourage other industrial countries to build up their stocks and to coordinate their use in a crisis. President Reagan, with support from Prime Ministers Margaret Thatcher and Yasuhiro Nakasone, obtained agreement on that strategy at the London economic summit of 1984. At present the U.S. reserve is 535 million barrels, Japan has 160 million barrels, and Germany 170 million barrels. Other countries are committed to build their stocks as well. In the event of an oil disruption the IEA countries can use their reserves to add as much as 4 to 5 mmbd to the oil market. If the disruption is sizable, the reserves should be used early to dampen upward price pressures. The world also has 9 to 10 mmbd of spare oil production capacity. Consequently, I do not see an energy security problem in the near term. As dependence on Persian Gulf oil increases, inventories of stocks should increase. I believe the OECD countries should build up their reserves so that they could add as much as 5 to 6 mmbd to the market by the mid-1990s.

The administration has also been concerned about Western European dependence on Soviet natural gas. In 1982 President Reagan expressed three worries: first, that Western Europe was subsidizing the pipeline carrying Siberian gas to Western Europe by providing low-interest credits to the Soviet Union; second, that some aspects of the technology transfer involved in constructing the Siberian gas pipeline could be disadvantageous to the United States; and third, that Western Europe could become so dependent on Siberian gas that the USSR would be able to exert political leverage by threatening to cut it off.

In the U.S.–Western European negotiations that followed our expression of these concerns, some helpful agreements were reached. OECD countries placed credits to the USSR on a fully commercial instead of a subsidized basis. And new efforts were initiated to encourage the development of the huge Troll natural gas field in the Norwegian section of the North Sea. That field is now being developed. As a result, Western Europe's dependence on Soviet natural gas will be limited, and Western energy security thereby strengthened.

In Central America, where half of export earnings must go to finance oil imports, the United States has undertaken to transfer technology to develop indigenous energy resources. The objective is to reduce long-term dependence on costly imported oil. The program is good for Central America, good for the world oil market, and ultimately helpful to U.S. energy security.

The recently negotiated Canadian Free Trade Agreement, now going through the ratification process, is another example of an international initiative that will have strong payoffs in energy security.

The agreement will remove all barriers to energy trade between the two countries, in sharp contrast to the 1970s, when Canada restricted oil and gas exports to the United States at the very time that energy security concerns were at their height. Particularly helpful in the area of natural gas, which can be a growing substitute for oil imports, the agreement will ensure that trade in natural gas will be fair and free and will benefit industry and strengthen energy security in both countries.

Energy policy was also discussed in the U.S.-Soviet summit in Geneva in 1985. The Soviets proposed expanding international collaboration in magnetic fusion science. The USSR has extensive experience in fusion research, as do the United States, Japan, and Western Europe. At a time when research budgets are constrained everywhere, and building new and larger machines costs more, such collaboration seems sensible, and President Reagan and General Secretary Mikhail Gorbachev agreed to cooperate.

Energy has also been important in U.S.-Japanese ties. In November 1983 President Reagan and Prime Minister Nakasone agreed to try to reduce the U.S. trade deficit by encouraging increased U.S. exports of coal, oil, and natural gas. Coal has the largest potential. Not much progress has been made, but the effort is still under way.

All these initiatives demonstrate the prominence accorded to energy in the policies of the Reagan administration. There is no easy route to energy security. It will not be realized through an oil import fee, or by subsidizing uneconomic projects, or by a solitary effort by the United States. Nonetheless, we are strengthening long-term energy security by actions in many fields, seemingly unrelated but in fact part of an integrated approach: negotiating the Free Trade Agreement with Canada, building emergency reserve stocks with allies, developing new technology to burn coal more cleanly, developing the Troll natural gas field in the North Sea, trying to preserve stripper production in Texas and strengthening the domestic oil and gas industry generally, and sponsoring basic research to support energy conservation and production. Recently in Savannah, Georgia, I toured a plant that produces electricity from waste. The project helped to solve a landfill problem and at the same time provide cost-effective electricity to the community. This project is also part of the mosaic for energy security.

We are not at the beginning but in the midst of a transition from a less to a more energy-secure world. We have learned important lessons, often the hard way, and earned important victories. The situation today is certainly energy secure.

There are warning signs on the horizon. They should be faced with full awareness of the uncertainty of energy projections and a recognition that the problem requires a long-term, not a crash, approach.

Discussion

Salvatore Lazzari noted that in a recent study, William Hogan of Harvard University criticized the DOE energy security study for grossly overestimating the macroeconomic costs of a $10 a barrel oil import tariff.[1] Hogan argues that the DOE study assumes the economy never adjusts to the tariff but simply goes on suffering the initial costs.

Martin replied that in Hogan's study energy is the top national concern and adverse consequences in other sectors are expected to meet energy security objectives. Hogan's macroeconomic costs are smaller than those calculated by DOE, partly because most of the revenues from an oil import fee are assumed to be recycled back to the economy. That calculation would be different if revenues were assumed to be used to reduce the deficit. DOE's analysis indicates that a $10 a barrel import fee would at best increase U.S. domestic oil production by 1.0 mmbd and reduce U.S. oil consumption by 0.5 mmbd by 1995, a drop in U.S. oil imports of 1.5 mmbd from what they otherwise would be. That would bring economic benefits in the form of some downward pressure on world oil prices. The cost, however, would be higher general price levels and lower economic

1. William W. Hogan and Bijan Mossavar-Rahmani, *Energy Security Revisited* (Harvard University, Energy and Environmental Policy Center, 1987), app. C, p. 32ff.

output paid year after year. When these costs are weighed against the benefits, an oil import fee does not look like a good proposition.

In the event of a severe oil supply disruption, the projected reduction in U.S. oil imports, say from 8 mmbd to 6 mmbd in 1995, would not mean much with the world oil market threatening to go out of control. None of these calculations, furthermore, takes into account the messy foreign policy realities. Canada, Mexico, and other nations would ask for exemption from the import fee, the net effect being to reduce the revenues while leaving the macroeconomic costs unaffected.

Franklin Salisbury asked whether the Department of Energy subsidized the Savannah treatment plant. He noted that many local municipalities face similar energy problems, and he wondered what DOE was doing to help.

Martin said no subsidies were necessary. The Savannah sanitation department agreed to pay the power producer eight dollars for every ton of trash it collected. The power producer built the treatment plant based on that guarantee, plus the rate it could charge for power. The plant meets all EPA requirements.

Taylor Kelsch asked whether Martin's injunction against unilateral U.S. action could be reconciled with Schlesinger's point, earlier in the day, that the essence of energy security is to preserve the U.S. capacity for independent action.

Martin said that no one country could resolve the problem of growing dependence on Persian Gulf oil. Any nation that draws increasingly on that oil supply is putting all nations at risk. Hence the need for coordination of energy policies among the OECD countries. He did not disagree with Schlesinger's point that increased U.S. dependence on foreign oil could reduce U.S. foreign policy flexibility. That is also a concern for Western Europe and Japan. We are all in a comfortable oil security position today, and we want to keep it that way. By the mid-1990s, however, as much as half the world's oil will come from the Persian Gulf region. That will reduce policy flexibility and is one of the factors that must be weighed today in deciding how much to increase energy stocks.

Edward Cowan asked when the administration hoped to meet its SPR goal of 750 million barrels.

Martin said the president notified Congress that he supported a fill rate of 100,000 barrels a day, which would mean reaching the goal of 750 million barrels by 1993. The president also said that money to purchase this oil would have to come from offsetting reductions in other budget expenditures. It is up to Congress to find those offsets.

Martin recalled that he once suggested financing the addition to the SPR by a one cent a gallon tax on gasoline. Other departments quickly suggested financing some of their important unmet goals the same way, showing how quickly the situation could get out of hand. That is one reason President Reagan is opposed to any tax increase. Energy security is important, but so are other national initiatives. With a shrinking budget, the trade-offs get harder. OMB insists on rigorous cost-benefit analyses, which take into account an appropriate discount rate. At a discount rate of, say, 10 percent, a dollar spent today to reduce the risk of a possible problem in 1995 is a much more costly expenditure than it seems.

Cowan also asked the administration's view on a variable levy on oil imports.

Martin said a variable import fee is just a backdoor way into a fixed oil import fee. It would do little to solve the energy security problem. DOE opposes it.

William Whitsit asked whether enhanced oil recovery research was underfunded in comparison with the $2.5 billion to be spent on coal technology. At present, he pointed out, two-thirds of the oil in a field is left in the ground when production is stopped.

Martin agreed that more funding is needed for enhanced oil recovery research, which is particularly important for the independent oil producers, and DOE is examining how this might be done. He explained that the funding for clean coal research is a special case. Clean coal is needed to relieve the acid rain problem. The alternative would be to install present-day technology scrubbers on coal-burning power plants at a cost of hundreds of billions of dollars. In cost-benefit terms, developing successful clean coal technology at a cost of $2.5 billion, shared with industry, would be a bargain.

Hendrik Houthakker commented that he was surprised to hear Martin treating the variable and fixed oil import levy in the same way. He favors a variable import fee with a low trigger price to give the U.S. oil industry some insurance against worst-case downside risks in the next few years.

Wilfred Kohl noted that after DOE's energy security report was released, the president sent a message to Congress asking for action on the proposals recommended in the report. What has happened and what remains to be done?

Martin said the president asked for deregulation of natural gas prices, the clean coal program, nuclear licensing reform, funds to increase the SPR to 750 million barrels, and removal of the windfall profit tax, among other things. The list was long. Congress has done nothing, which is a source of frustration. A sound energy policy requires an energy consensus, which we still need to develop. Some complain that more action is needed than has been proposed. That is no reason to delay action on measures that are cost-effective, consistent with sound economic principles, and beneficial to national security. Once those measures are under way, we can better assess whether more is needed.

In his letter to Congress the president said that if oil prices were to collapse or if conditions in the industry were to deteriorate further, he might propose further action. At this point, the administration is well ahead in the debate, waiting for others to catch up.

Public Policy Choices

JAMES A. McCLURE

Preparing for Emergencies

In formulating energy policy, it should be taken for granted that energy problems in future emergencies will look different from the way they look now. For example, in the spring of 1973 I was giving a speech in Dallas on energy. I said at the time that the price of oil could well go above $5 a barrel. I also said that the availability of oil might depend on other than economic events or factors. Both points were greeted with considerable disbelief.

Not long afterward, a political event—the Arab oil embargo—and several years later another political event—the Iranian revolution—disrupted the supply of energy. As a result, the price of oil moved from less than $2 a barrel on the East Coast of the United States to well over $30 a barrel. These prices applied to the same commodity, from the same sources, going into the same market. That noneconomic events can shape the availability of energy has become a fact of life and a national security concern of the Western industrialized democracies.

I am not going to predict that similar political events will happen soon. But to believe they are not possible is to be oblivious to the news. Indeed, I have been surprised that markets have responded as little as they have to the tanker war in the Persian Gulf. Two factors probably account for this comparative market stability. One is the existence of a strategic petroleum reserve (SPR) in the United States amounting to over 500 million barrels of oil. The other is the expressed willingness of the United States to use this reserve to dampen short-term swings in supply. Both factors are important and together can indeed dampen short-term swings in supply. I want to emphasize dampen and short term. The SPR cannot be used for very long and therefore cannot deal with long-term supply questions. It is not the answer to all our energy problems.

For those who believe that market forces will allocate everything perfectly in the event of a disruption, I point to 1973 and to 1979 and assert that, theory notwithstanding, Congress will not leave the responsibility for dealing with an emergency solely to market forces. For those who believe that government intervention will only make matters worse, I have few words of comfort. Rest assured that the government will intervene. It is of course hypothetically possible that the government will stay out of it. But I am here to tell you, having been there twice before and having some expertise in politics, that the government will intervene in an energy emergency and will make matters worse.

Therefore, in considering the range of options for dealing with oil supply emergencies, one can rule out leaving it to the market. That leads me to believe we ought to have some kind of rational emergency authority on the shelf. It should be put in place in dispassionate times for use in more passionate times when shortages exist, the phone is ringing off the wall, and every special interest group in the United States is pleading its cause for having favored access to petroleum supplies.

I also believe that a range of policies, not a single policy, is necessary. There should be policies to ensure adequate research and development, to provide for market testing, and even to proceed with activities that the marketplace would not justify in normal times, because of the effects of political events occurring in the Middle East. For example, I would be hesitant to invest in the production of oil in the United States if nothing existed to moderate the effects of such unexpected political events on that investment. Yet it is important to make such investments possible in this country. We ought to have public land management policies that make public resources available for market investment and exploration if such investments are economic. I refer specifically to exploration in the outer continental shelf. It is wrong for the United States to place its best oil prospects off limits as though it were self-sufficient and had no need to worry about its oil supply.

I am also amazed that with a tanker war going on in the Persian Gulf debate in Congress focuses on why the president chose to reflag the Kuwaiti tankers rather than use some other option. We should be talking about an energy policy to ensure the supply of oil in the future, not debating the finer points of the U.S. response in the Persian Gulf.

I could choose some other responses rather than reflagging.

Perhaps the president would have been wise to call the leadership of Congress together, explain the situation, lay out alternatives, and ask for suggestions. Energy should be a partnership policy. A long-term policy not shared and supported by both parties will be subjected to endless nitpicking and will ultimately fail. The American public sees little reason to think about oil supply emergencies when supplies now are more than ample. In this situation, instituting a long-term energy policy requires bipartisan leadership and support.

I do not know how much of the world's poor economic performance in the 1980s was caused by the profound changes in energy prices. But I suspect that a large part grew out of the price jump and price collapse after 1979. Not all countries, of course, reacted in the same way. Japan, though much more dependent on imported energy than the United States, quickly made the adjustments that allowed it to compensate for the change and remain competitive in the world. It was able to discipline itself to improve productivity in the face of higher energy costs in ways that the United States and many Western European countries were unable to do. Other Pacific-area countries like Korea, Taiwan, and China also did a better job of adjusting to higher energy costs than the United States did, despite our comparatively favorable energy position. And indeed, this growing competition in the Pacific is a general economic phenomenon of this decade with which we will have to deal.

To sum up, there are a range of policies that should be explored, and the government is talking about them. The Arctic National Wildlife Preserve is opening up. The Department of the Interior is moving forward with the outer continental shelf leasing program. So far there seems to be no desire on the part of Congress to interfere this year, because nothing has happened yet. It is only when action is imminent that Congress feels compelled to step in and stop it. The United States continues to invest heavily in coal R&D. It continues to invest in conservation. There is a growing sentiment on Capitol Hill in favor of alcohol as a fuel. And Congress continues to try to improve the prospects for nuclear energy, for example by trying to get legislation passed to settle the issue of nuclear radioactive waste storage. I am confident that nuclear energy will come back as an important energy component in our future. It is in every other major country.

As to other proposals commonly discussed, I do not support an import fee, though I might support a minimum price to take the downside market risk out of oil investment. Such a minimum price would stimulate some investment that otherwise might not occur under the threat of a price collapse. In any event, I believe any price collapse would be short term. OPEC is likely to act to prevent another free fall in the price. The Saudis have demonstrated their ability to discipline that organization if need be.

More generally, I believe the U.S. government faces several policy choices. It could artificially raise the price of oil and oil products, thereby stimulating the development of alternatives. Or through subsidies of one kind or another, it could choose to stimulate the alternatives without artificially raising the price of oil. Or it could choose to avoid intervention and let the market do the job of allocating and developing resources.

Available information shows fairly conclusively that U.S. oil consumption will increase, the U.S. oil production base will decline, and U.S. oil imports will rise. In this situation, we may find it preferable to seek a gradual, rather than permit a convulsive, transition to the next phase in energy. In any event, that is the nature of the choice we will have to face.

PHILIP R. SHARP

A Practical Energy Policy for the 1990s

Much of the disagreement over public policy choices required to deal with the "energy problem" results from confusion over what the problem is. If the problem is defined as one of immediately restoring and maintaining the health of the domestic oil industry, one set of choices makes sense. If the problem is defined more broadly as energy security, of which the health of the domestic oil industry is only a part, though an important part, different choices are suggested.

Narrow perspectives on energy can be dangerous. The topic of this conference, Oil and America's Security, seems broad, but in fact limiting our focus to oil or to America can result in flawed policy choices. Too narrow a definition can lead to such inconsistencies as the Department of Energy's support for tax incentives for oil and gas production and opposition to tax incentives for conservation and renewables. An equally unhelpful definition of the problem is one that focuses only on U.S. oil imports, ignoring supply and demand elsewhere that help set world and therefore U.S. prices; that type of definition can lead to such grossly erroneous policy choices as an oil import fee.

The problem of energy security—broadly defined—is a *potential* one. Policymakers often talk of the coming energy crisis as if it were a foregone conclusion. Such exaggeration or misplaced certainty may be useful in combatting our national grasshopper attitude about energy. But it can also lead to crisis-mentality solutions that impose unnecessary costs on the consumer, the U.S. Treasury, or the environment. Most of the country and the world are enjoying today's low energy prices. Because low prices increase demand and reduce production, however, the United States and the rest of the world are likely to become too heavily dependent on a few Persian Gulf nations in the next decade.

DANGEROUS TRENDS

A set of worrisome trends causes many policymakers to conclude that the question is not whether, but when, there will be another oil crisis. Relatively cheap prices have discouraged conservation and cut U.S. oil production by 700,000 barrels a day in 1986 and cumulatively by 1 mmbd in 1987. U.S. oil import dependency went from 27 percent to about 34 percent in just two years (from 4.3 mmbd in 1985 to 5.3 mmbd in 1987). The inevitable decline in Prudhoe Bay, North Sea, and much other non-OPEC production, coupled with increasing world demand, could restore monopoly power in the next several years to a handful of Persian Gulf countries, where it still costs only $1 to produce a barrel and where a growing percentage of the world's reserves remain.

These trends are dangerous and seem irreversible, leading many forecasters to predict a 55–60 percent U.S. dependence on oil imports in the 1990s. A doubling of 1986 prices and a 50 percent increase in 1986 imports, not a farfetched possibility, would lead to a threefold increase in the 1986 net oil import bill of $28 billion, a staggering economic threat. Such a scenario cannot be taken lightly.

COUNTER TRENDS

Before reacting precipitously, however, we should recall how wrong previous predictions have been and we should not neglect a few factors that could make the future different from the past. For example, the United States now has a strategic petroleum reserve of more than 530 million barrels, and other countries are building their reserves. The decontrol of oil and gas prices has largely ended the artificial overconsumption and underproduction of the 1970s, allowing both producers and consumers to anticipate and therefore mitigate a price shock. Interfuel substitutability has increased dramatically, particularly in industry. Large world gas discoveries in the 1970s and a 40 percent increase in natural gas consumption in the 1980s have helped slow the increase in oil demand.

Improvements in efficiency continue, though at a slower rate, largely because of the gains in automobile and industrial efficiency begun in the 1970s that are still moving into the economy. New pipelines bypassing the Persian Gulf have reduced the possibility of cutting off exports by blocking the Strait of Hormuz. Recent additions to Venezuela's heavy oil reserves (not officially proven but claimed to be recoverable with today's technology and prices) are more than five times the size of all U.S. oil reserves.

On a less tangible level, the realization by the Saudis and other rational OPEC powers that too great a price rise can reduce their revenues over time, and the perception by consuming nations' policymakers that energy troubles could recur, may help prevent shocks like those of 1973–74 and 1979–80.

As we attempt to map our energy future for the next decade and beyond, we should therefore not mark our charts as the Renaissance cartographers marked the unexplored oceans, "Here Be Dragons," but rather we should acknowledge uncertainty and the need for caution by using their term for unexplored land, *terra incognita*.

THREE THREATS TO ENERGY SECURITY

John Lichtblau has drawn a useful distinction between a crisis, "a sudden, extraordinary, time-limited dislocation of major proportions," and worrisome longer-term trends and developments such as the potential effect of a growing level of import dependency on prices, trade balances, foreign policy, and national security.[1] For purposes of analyzing public policy choices to meet threats to U.S. energy security, a third, longer-term concern should be added, and a distinction made among the three principal types of threat:

1. Disruption—a short-term cutoff of oil supplies, such as might be caused by a broader war in the Middle East or a politically, religiously, or economically motivated cutback in production.

2. Long-term supply and demand squeeze—a tighter world oil market brought about by reduced production capacity and increased world consumption, again giving a few Persian Gulf nations the ability to set world energy prices and wreak economic havoc by reducing or increasing production.

1. "Introductory Remarks," Petroleum Industry Research Foundation, Oil Policy Seminar, Washington, D.C., September 29, 1987.

3. "Greenhouse" short—a potential requirement to move to a post-fossil energy world on a massive and rapid basis if worst-case scenarios of the greenhouse effect and global warming prove to be true.

Although two or more of these threats could occur simultaneously and compound their effect, each requires different, though not immediately incompatible, policy choices. None is strictly a U.S. problem; each one must be tackled by all the major energy consumer nations. Because the United States is the world's largest energy consumer, however, all U.S. policy choices are important both symbolically and in reality.

THE POLITICAL CLIMATE

These policy choices cannot be made by experts in a seminar; they must take into account the prevailing political winds. Experts can and should warn a complacent public of potential danger ahead, as should political leaders, but actions have to be based on public support.

Support for any significant action in energy today is thin. Although the energy-producing sector of the economy is experiencing serious difficulties, most of the country is enjoying today's low energy prices. Warnings that an energy problem might occur in the next decade are not likely to move a public that is rarely willing to sacrifice in the present to pay for future benefits.

In refusing to buy the high-option energy insurance policy—oil import fees, massive government expenditures, high prices now to avoid future high prices—the public is not wrong. Although taking no action would be irresponsible, there is little intellectual basis for massive government intervention to promote energy security.

We have learned from painful experience that it is difficult to forecast energy prices or demand, and we are now learning that it is expensive to be wrong on the high side as well as the low side. We paid too little attention to energy security in the 1960s, taking cheap energy for granted, and we suffered for it in the 1970s. But we tried to do too much on a crash basis in the 1970s in anticipation of high prices and demand that never occurred, and we have paid a huge price in this decade in the form of misplaced investments (for example, synthetic fuels expenditures, deep gas, oil development, and loans premised on $50 a barrel prices, liquified natural gas imports, and excess electricity capacity).[2]

Just as the underinvestment in energy in the 1960s led to tenfold price increases and huge economic dislocations in the 1970s, the overinvestment in energy in the late 1970s and early 1980s is causing economic losses for society now. Legislators and regulators are struggling in several arenas to figure out how to allocate the costs of these overinvestments. Our inability to answer these questions, combined with the once-burned-twice-shy phenomenon and Wall Street's desire for quick results, may be causing underinvestment in energy now. This is likely to lead to the next generation of problems— how to allocate the costs that will result from our current underinvestment (that is, shortages or high prices) and crash programs to catch up in the 1990s.

In addition, most government actions to promote energy security will conflict with other goals of society, chiefly deficit reduction, tax simplification, low consumer prices, regulatory relief, or environmental protection. During a period of widely shared concern about energy, such as the late 1970s, achievement of these other values can sometimes be sacrificed to energy security. In a period of energy complacency, though, the political forces arguing for these other goals will usually prevail.

The present administration has difficulty in countering this low public ranking of energy security goals because of inconsistency and the absence of a well-conceived and well-articulated policy. Administration officials regularly call for selected actions to promote energy security, but the lack of balance in the proposals diminishes their effectiveness. When the issue is leasing in the Arctic National Wildlife Refuge and the outer continental shelf, or nuclear research, or tax incentives for oil production, these officials argue that energy security should override budgetary or environmental concerns. But when the issue is the strategic petroleum reserve, alternative fuels, conservation, or research and development, energy security becomes less important than the budget or antigovernment ideology.

2. For a fuller discussion, see Philip R. Sharp, "The World Oil Outlook: A Congressional Perspective," *Forum for Applied Research and Public Policy*, vol. 2 (Fall 1987).

ENERGY POLICY GOALS

The key goals of an appropriate U.S. energy policy for the 1990s should be stockpiles, diversity, and flexibility. The United States and other consuming countries should build adequate stockpiles to discourage or to cushion the effects of a short-term interruption of oil supplies. We should increasingly rely on a diversity of energy sources, both fuels and nations. We should seek flexibility so we can quickly and efficiently switch away from, or conserve, a fuel in short supply, reducing the lead time and the cost of making such changes when they are justified by price.

CRITERIA FOR JUDGING ENERGY POLICY

What would constitute an intellectually respectable, politically acceptable energy policy? It would seek a balance between the risks of overinvestment and underinvestment. It would avoid laissez-faire complacency at the same time that it would reject crash programs designed to achieve immediate results, focusing rather on a series of relatively inexpensive, nonintrusive, and environmentally benign actions that collectively can make a difference in the longer term. It would recognize the equal value of increased production and decreased demand. It would focus on world supply and demand, recognizing that world prices set U.S. prices, and focus on all resources, recognizing that a French nuclear plant, a Japanese advance in photovoltaics, and a U.S. improvement in automobile fuel efficiency all contribute to a reduction of world oil demand.

COMPONENTS OF A FEASIBLE ENERGY POLICY

Although a forward-looking, politically acceptable energy policy is easier to describe in the abstract than in specifics, let me suggest a few actions that might qualify. Some are directed more at a short-term disruption, others at longer-term supply and demand and the greenhouse effect. It is not an all-inclusive list, and all proposals are not equal in importance or cost, but none is insignificant or politically impossible with adequate leadership.

—Provide secure funding for the strategic petroleum reserve and fill it rapidly. There is no better investment we can make in energy security, and the funding should not be subjected every year to the vagaries of the budget process. The administration's endorsement early in 1987 of a 100,000 barrel a day fill rate, but only if Congress could find offsetting spending cuts, was a disgrace. That is not the way the president endorsed Star Wars funding or aid for the contras. Following serious criticism of its halfhearted approach, the administration has now amended its budget to make an honest request for the funds, an encouraging sign. Coordination with other industrial oil-consuming nations on reserve building and early drawdown policies is also important; in this area the administration deserves high marks.

—Encourage the adoption of substitutes for gasoline and diesel fuel, which are responsible for half of U.S. oil consumption and one out of eight barrels of oil consumed in the world today. This is the single most important step we can take now to affect oil demand and prices. We can do this by providing incentives through the corporate average fuel efficiency (CAFE) standard for auto manufacturers to build methanol, ethanol, compressed natural gas, or other nonpetroleum cars. As the DOE energy security study pointed out, the United States could reduce oil imports by about a million barrels a day by converting 10 percent of its vehicles, a realistic goal.[3] But as the study did not point out, it is necessary to provide some limited incentives immediately if we expect to achieve these results in this century. H.R. 3399, a bipartisan bill to do this, is moving through the House, and Senator Jay Rockefeller and others have introduced similar legislation in the Senate.

—Promote the use of America's abundant energy resource: conservation and efficiency. A barrel of oil conserved through improved efficiency is more valuable than a barrel produced, because it is likely to be repeated year after year—the gift that keeps on giving. The Department of Energy's budget request for conservation for fiscal year 1988 is only 11 percent of the fiscal year 1981 appropriation. Although we have made great improvements in energy efficiency and conservation already (average household use of energy dropped

3. U.S. Department of Energy, *Energy Security: A Report to the President of the United States* (GPO, 1987).

13 percent and industrial use of energy per unit of output declined 22 percent between 1975 and 1984), there is still much cost-effective conservation to be "produced." The Germans, French, and Japanese use roughly half the energy per capita that we do, and their economies are not suffering.[4] The appliance efficiency standards legislation enacted this year is a perfect example of a cheap, nonintrusive, environmentally benign step that can make a big difference in energy demand in the future. Congress is exploring the possibility of standards for other major appliances, including fluorescent lighting ballasts and plumbing fixtures, as well as other conservation initiatives. Adequate funding for weatherization programs will also pay off in long-term demand reduction and serve important social goals.

—Promote the cleaner, more efficient use of America's most abundant fuel, coal, by demonstrating clean coal technologies. The president's proposal to spend $2.5 billion to meet the goals of the U.S.-Canadian Envoys' report on acid rain is a positive development, but the large funding commitment and the lack of a clear focus on emissions reduction jeopardize the program's ultimate success. Acid-rain controls, if not carefully tailored, could add to our energy security and trade problems by significantly raising the cost of coal use and encouraging more oil and gas use.

—Stop shortchanging energy research and development. Many of our recent gains in production and conservation are the result of previous R&D expenditures, but now we are in effect eating our seed corn. Although Congress has refused to accept all the administration's proposed cuts in the last six years, the United States is still spending less on relatively inexpensive R&D than the risk of future energy problems warrants. In addition to work on enhanced oil recovery, clean coal, and conservation, which can help with supply and demand in the near future, R&D in renewable energy, hydrogen, energy storage systems, superconductivity, and safe, economical nuclear power can make a difference in addressing twenty-first century problems such as the depletion of hydrocarbon reserves and the greenhouse effect.

—Make nuclear power a politically acceptable option by improving

4. Testimony of Arthur H. Rosenfeld, "Conservation and Competitiveness," House Budget Committee Task Force on Community and Natural Resources, July 15, 1987.

the government's and industry's performance and attitudes on safety. For us to avoid a situation in which public opposition forecloses any new nuclear construction and may shut down existing plants one by one, the public must have confidence in the commitment of industry and regulators to reactor safety and safe waste disposal. An essential first step is the appointment of officials at the Department of Energy and the Nuclear Regulatory Commission who are, and who are perceived to be, tough, objective servants of the public, not the industry. Continued research on designs for inherently safe reactors is also important, as is peer review of major government nuclear decisions and operations by independent scientists and engineers.

—Encourage a gradual transition to as much competition in the generation of electricity as is consistent with reliability of service. If the current disincentives to build new baseload generating capacity persist, utilities may become too reliant on gas turbines, which can be built relatively quickly and cheaply. Although this may help in reducing the reliance on long-term demand forecasts, it could also reduce diversity and may not be the least costly option in the long run. The government should encourage the industry to diversify its supply options for the 1990s to avoid higher prices for consumers and upward pressure on gas and oil prices. The Federal Energy Regulatory Commission's (FERC) recent proposals for competitive bidding on new generating capacity have started a useful dialogue in this area.

—Complete the decontrol of natural gas and the adoption of "contract carriage"—that is, the limitation of interstate pipelines to the transportation service. This can be accomplished only by ensuring that competition is available to all participants in the market and is not used as a way of sticking captive residential consumers with the costs of existing high-priced contracts. In today's market, consumer prices will not rise as a result of decontrol, but there is a corresponding diminished enthusiasm for complete decontrol among producers. Lingering regional differences and rigidities will make legislation exceptionally difficult, and the industry may have to stumble toward decontrol and open access through administrative actions. Recent FERC decisions, though still contested, have moved a long way along this rocky road.

—Resolve which of the most promising potential new oil and gas areas will be open for development and which will be kept off limits.

We cannot afford to close them all off indefinitely. We clearly need to weigh the energy benefits against the environmental costs in every case, but we may have to rank our environmental priorities. For example, even if the environmental costs are high, we may not be able to afford the luxury of blocking the development of the most productive areas of the California outer continental shelf *and* the Arctic National Wildlife Refuge *and* public lands throughout the West. A careful balancing is needed. For example, the ability of Robert Redford's Institute for Resource Management to reach a consensus among industry and environmental groups on some leasing issues in the Bering Sea was encouraging, but the Interior Department's rejection of the consensus position was not. The Reagan administration's continued reputation for antienvironmental bias eliminates any credibility it may have had in recommending an appropriate balance between energy and the environment.

—Provide limited tax incentives for oil and gas exploration. Repeal of the windfall profit tax, which now raises almost no revenue, would reduce producers' current paperwork costs and provide an incentive through higher potential rates of return. Those who are more knowledgeable can say which other incentives would be most useful and provide the most production bang for the revenue buck, but the tax breaks must go for exploration and new production rather than for corporate diversification or for production that would have occurred anyway. The goal is energy security, not income maintenance for the industry. To avoid a negative effect on the deficit, a small excise tax on all oil products could be designed to offset the revenue losses from production incentives.

—Continue to encourage energy trade with Canada and Mexico, countries that are as important from an energy perspective as any other. The recent free trade agreement proposed between Canada and the United States may serve as a beginning for a truly open energy trade, without protection or subsidies, between these two important partners. Canadian oil, gas, and electricity are relatively abundant and inexpensive, and we should use their proximity to fashion yet another weapon against the instability of foreign supplies from potentially less friendly and more volatile regions of the world.

All these steps are politically possible, but none will be easy to accomplish without strong leadership from the administration. The public concern necessary to create political momentum for action without such leadership is not yet present. Unfortunately, if we cannot achieve even these modest proposals by the time high prices cause a public outcry about energy, it may be too late for anything but crash programs.

WILLIAM A. NISKANEN

A Primer on Energy Security Policy

May I remind you of some simple truths about America's energy security. Although I am not the first or only person to recognize these truths, they are not yet broadly shared. Indeed, much current energy policy and most of the proposed changes in energy policy reflect, I believe, a fundamental misunderstanding of these issues.

I propose to spell out these issues in five points.

Number one. The energy security of the United States is not dependent on the level of our oil imports or, in turn, on the level of our domestic production. As long as governments allow the oil market to operate, the price of oil, exclusive of transportation charges, will be the same in all nations, whether they are wholly dependent on oil imports, such as Japan and Germany; partially dependent, such as the United States; or oil exporters, such as Mexico. In turn, the amount of oil consumed in any nation, including the United States, will depend on its respective demands at the then-available world price, regardless of the amount of the supply disruption.

It follows from this point that policies to increase the domestic production of oil or oil substitutes will not increase the nation's energy security. Therefore, the decision on such issues as opening additional offshore areas or Alaskan land to oil exploration and production should be based on the balancing of marketing and environmental concerns, but not on the false premise that such additional production will either reduce the price or increase the domestic availability of oil during a supply disruption.

Similarly, an oil import tax should be recognized as a "drain America first" policy that will increase current oil prices to American consumers and industries without providing any insurance against even higher prices in the future.

Number two. The energy security of the United States is not dependent on the source of its oil imports. A supply disruption in any region of the world will increase the price of oil to all nations by the same amount, independent of how much oil had been imported from that region. Similarly, the United States is not more secure because it purchases only a small share of its oil imports from the Middle East; reducing that share will not make it more secure.

Our government has correctly recognized that the U.S. economic stake in maintaining free transit of the Persian Gulf is a function of our total oil imports, not of our imports from that region. It does not appear to recognize, however, that the U.S. interest in free transit of the Gulf is shared by Iran, which is wholly dependent on use of the Gulf to export its oil. For reasons that are not clear to me, our current Gulf policy appears to be directed against Iran. There may be valid reasons for the anti-Iran tilt to this policy, but such reasons do not include energy security.

Number three. A political or military threat to the governments of the oil-producing countries would not necessarily reduce U.S. energy security. The energy security issue is whether such a threat would increase or reduce oil production from these countries. In fact, a reduction in the security of the property rights held by the current oil producers could well lead to increased current oil production and lower current oil prices.

Put yourself in the position of the Saudi royal family. They have, let us say, two assets in their portfolio: oil in the ground and U.S. government securities. Under current circumstances they choose to have so much in the U.S. government securities and so much in oil left in the ground. Suppose then that because of a change in the domestic or international situation the probability of their continuing to exercise effective property rights over oil in the ground one year from now goes down from 90 percent to 50 percent. They would then have stronger incentives to sell more oil so as to shift more of their assets to U.S. government securities in the West.

This type of reasoning motivated the Middle East production policies of the major oil companies from the Suez crisis of 1956 to the early 1970s, when the Gulf states asserted their rights to establish oil production levels. The Suez crisis demonstrated that although the oil companies had the right to pump, they would not have secure rights to the fields indefinitely. Consequently, they produced a steadily increasing volume, which in turn was the primary reason that the price of oil was unusually low for most of the period.

A change in government in oil-producing countries would probably have much the same effect. The United States may have valid reasons for avoiding the wealth transfer from current governments in oil-producing countries to other potential governments, but such reasons do not include energy security. If, for example, the Soviet Union took over one of the Middle Eastern states, the United States would lose in the sense that Soviet wealth would increase, but the volume of oil production by that country might very well rise.

It is not simply who owns the assets but the incentives of those who do that counts as far as energy security is concerned. Thus U.S. energy security would indeed be reduced as a consequence of the unification of the major oil-producing states, or by other measures that would produce effective enforcement of production limits, such as the physical destruction of the oil production and transit facilities. There are all kinds of political developments in the Middle East and elsewhere short of the physical destruction of the oil facilities or the unification of the oil-producing nations that may well be contrary to U.S. national interests, but they would not necessarily reduce our energy security. In sum, the relation between U.S. economic interests and political and military developments in the Middle East depends on the character of these developments.

Number four. The primary value of the main energy security policies developed by the oil-importing nations is that they reduce the prospects of a recurrence of earlier policy mistakes. In this regard, the International Energy Agency (IEA) and the strategic petroleum reserve deserve special attention.

The IEA was born out of the compulsion of politicians to be perceived to be doing something in response to a perceived problem. It is on the whole an innocuous agency. At one time there was some prospect that it might be important. It could have facilitated the establishment of a common external tariff on oil by the industrial nations, which would have recaptured much of the economic rent gained by OPEC. Such a policy, however, was never seriously considered.

The IEA oil-sharing agreement has little value. If implemented, it would lead to some waste in shipping costs, but in the end would not affect the allocation of oil among nations during a supply disruption.

Its one important provision is that member nations have committed themselves not to restrict exports or reexports of oil in the event of a selective embargo by oil-producing countries. In effect, they will not facilitate the enforcement of such an embargo but instead will allow the international oil market to operate. The member governments could have made the same commitment without creating the IEA, but the salary of a few bureaucrats is a small price to pay to keep it in force.

Creation of the strategic petroleum reserve is another example of the cost of earlier policy mistakes, mistakes that Senator McClure has assured us will again be made. In a world in which governments make a credible commitment to avoid imposing price controls or windfall profit taxes, there is no obvious reason why private firms would not provide a sufficient stock of oil for emergencies. This is not the world in which we live. As a result, private firms will not provide a sufficient stock of oil, and some government investment in a strategic petroleum reserve is desirable. Moreover, the perception that this reserve is sufficient to avoid temporary shortages until the oil market adjusts to the supply disruption should reduce the political pressure for price controls and allocations during the next supply disruption. Thus it may also reduce the substitution of public for private oil stocks.

To repeat, the expense of building this strategic petroleum reserve could have been avoided if the government had not previously imposed price controls and windfall profit taxes on oil. Now that the reserve has been accumulated, the cost of maintaining it is a small price to pay for avoiding recurrence of these policies.

There are two issues concerning the reserve that remain to be addressed. First, the Department of Energy has not yet determined or announced the rules under which oil from the reserve would be released, thereby creating unnecessary uncertainty for private firms. Second, the case for the continued expansion of this reserve is far from clear.

Number five. My final point is by way of a summary. The best ensurance of energy security would be a mutual agreement by OECD governments to avoid interference in national and international energy markets. Secure property rights in the OECD countries and a commitment to avoid price controls, allocations, windfall profit taxes, and restraints on either imports or exports would be the best means of dealing with unpleasant contingencies arising elsewhere in the world that we can neither forecast nor wholly control.

At the same time there is no obvious case for the several current tax preferences or subsidies to develop and produce either oil or oil substitutes.

There are valid reasons to be concerned about the health, safety and environmental effects of the production and use of different types of energy. These concerns should not be overridden in the name of energy security.

The United States may have valid reasons for concern about the political and military conditions in the Middle East, but some changes in those conditions are not necessarily contrary to U.S. energy security interests.

MACK WALLACE

A Perilous Choice:
Minesweepers or Drilling Rigs

In 1986 foreign oil-producing countries flooded world oil markets and drove prices below $10 a barrel. This price collapse severely damaged America's strategic domestic oil- and gas-producing industry. Nevertheless, I believe it can be repaired if timely action is taken. Specifically, imposing a *variable* fee on imports of crude oil and refined petroleum products would go a long way toward enabling the oil-producing industry in this country to rehabilitate itself.

U.S. OIL PRODUCTION POTENTIAL

Before the 1986 price collapse, aggressive drilling had arrested the nearly decade-long production decline of the mid-1970s and early 1980s in Texas as well as in the other lower forty-eight states. Drillers, motivated by price levels existing from 1979 through 1985, located new reserves in the lower forty-eight states at a rate equal to production. And production, to the surprise of many people, was itself essentially stabilized. This experience showed that the U.S. oil and gas resource base could provide relatively stable levels of production well into the next century.

The January 1986 oil price crash jeopardized that stability. I am confident that the domestic exploration and producing industry can once again be revitalized. But that will not happen until the potential for price gyrations such as those of the past year have been eliminated and prices high enough to ensure a stable environment for investment in the industry have been established. The president and Congress have the instruments at hand to provide the needed help. I urge that they be put to use.

DAMAGE TO THE OIL AND GAS INDUSTRY

The precipitous decline in oil field exploration in the United States reflects the seriousness of the industry's current difficulties. This decline is shown in the U.S. "rig count," a figure indicating the number of rotary drilling rigs in operation and published weekly by the Baker Hughes Company.

In 1986 the rig count averaged about one-half that of 1985 (963 as against 1,980). In July 1986 it had dropped below 700, lower than any time since record keeping began in the early 1940s. By the fourth quarter of 1987 the rig count rose to about 1,100, a level that is still greatly depressed. Exploration budgets have been sharply reduced, rigs are rusting, and geologists are leaving the industry. In sum, the infrastructure is being severely eroded.[1]

The United States may not necessarily need a return to the 3,000 to 4,000 rig level of 1980–82, though that would contribute greatly to the energy independence of the nation. At a minimum, however, activity at 1984–85 levels, or twice the present number, is necessary (figure 1).

The present period resembles that of the late 1960s and early 1970s, when U.S. oil reserves and production declined at alarming rates. As a result, the United States became increasingly dependent on foreign energy supplies, which contributed to the imposition of the Arab oil embargo in 1973. We cannot afford to let that happen again.

U.S. oil production is already down significantly because of the fall in oil prices. Between January 1986 and September 1987 total production (including natural gas liquids) declined from 10.9 mmbd to 9.9 mmbd.

The rate of decline varies by state and by area. In those parts of the United States where a large percentage of production is from marginal stripper wells, average annual loss of production exceeds 12 percent and in 1987 January through December declines exceeded 20 percent. Prime examples are North Texas, Oklahoma, and Kansas,

---

1. Ironically, we are now suffering from a glut of natural gas—or at least the appearance of a surplus. Demand continues to decline (in part because cheap oil imports are "backing out" gas). But so does our natural gas delivery capability, since it is dependent on continued drilling. We need to put rigs back to work developing this significant resource.

FIGURE 1. *Annual Average U.S. Active Rotary Rigs, 1940–86*

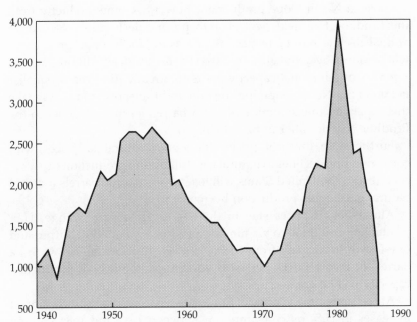

as well as the Rocky Mountain states. Areas of the lower forty-eight states in which reserve growth had been strong during the 1980s— for example, the Permian Basin of West Texas—were less hard hit. Stable production in the outer continental shelf and a small increase in Alaskan production held the net loss in annual U.S. production to 0.7 mmbd between 1985 and 1987.

If the price of oil stays in the $15 to $20 a barrel range, the outlook for U.S. oil production through 1990 is poor. Severely reduced cash flow will continue to curtail oil drilling, both for reserve growth and new field discovery, yielding a corresponding loss of reserve additions.

In the lower forty-eight states, additions to reserves nearly equaled production over the past five years. The reduction in drilling at a $15 price would result in forgone reserve additions and an estimated total production loss of about 1.7 mmbd for the period 1988–90. These reductions would leave a 1990 annual production level for the lower forty-eight estimated at just under 4.8 mmbd.

Alaskan North Slope production, now 1.875 mmbd, chiefly from the Prudhoe Bay field, will go into normal decline in 1988. At an annual decline rate of 12 percent, Alaskan North Slope production will be down by about 400,000 barrels a day by 1990. Although about 1 mmbd of additional capacity exists in already discovered, smaller fields on the North Slope, production and transportation costs make this capability uneconomical at $15 a barrel, so that no offset to the Prudhoe Bay decline can be anticipated.

Furthermore, lower oil prices will depress natural gas prices, with corresponding declines in natural gas drilling and production capacity. As a result, the United States will lose about 350,000 barrels a day of natural gas liquids production by 1990.

Altogether, if prices stay in the $15 to $20 a barrel range, U.S. production could fall to 7.5 mmbd, a loss of 2.5 mmbd in output and one-fourth in capacity from the 1987 level. If prices fall below $15 a barrel, or if low prices persist beyond 1990, the loss of production capacity will be greater.

At the same time, a price of $15 to $20 a barrel will mean continued increases in U.S. oil consumption. Between 1982 and 1985 U.S. oil consumption stabilized at about 15.5 mmbd after marked declines earlier. But U.S. demand for petroleum in 1986 was up 3 percent over 1985, to 16.2 mmbd, and by an estimated 2 percent in 1987. Imports in 1987 averaged more than 6 mmbd, or about 40 percent of consumption.

By 1990 demand could be between 16.5 and 17.5 mmbd. During 1989 imports could reach 50 percent of supply, exceeding the all-time historical high reached in 1977. If production continues to decline at current rates, imports could constitute *two-thirds* of supply in the mid-1990s. The United States should act now to prevent import dependence at this scale from becoming a reality.

STRATEGIC CONSIDERATIONS

Oil's strategic character is self-evident. Modern conventional war cannot be waged without it. In peacetime, as the *Oil and Gas Journal* put it editorially, "Petroleum remains the cheapest, most versatile, and—consequently—most strategically important fuel." In light of its strategic importance, how can the United States permit itself to become dependent on foreign sources for 50 percent of its needs by 1990 and perhaps two-thirds dependent by 1995? An increasing proportion of these imports, furthermore, will have to be met from unstable if not volatile areas of the Middle East.

How short is our memory? The Arab oil embargo in 1973–74 caused a disruption of supply, political tremors, and a price shock. The Iranian revolution culminating in the fall of the shah of Iran and the assumption of power by the Ayatollah Khomeini caused prices in 1979–80 to double once again. Indeed, oil's significance is such that the Carter administration apparently may have considered the use of tactical nuclear weapons to prevent the vast, cheaply exploitable reserves of the Persian Gulf from falling into Soviet hands.[2]

In view of the importance of oil to the domestic economy, will the United States be able to conduct foreign policy independent of concerns about imports? Or—since 75 percent of the world's oil is owned by governments that have no reluctance to use it as an instrument of foreign policy—will U.S. policies be hostage to the whims of rulers in the Middle East? In the end, growing dependence on foreign oil will compromise independence in the formulation of U.S. foreign policy.

POLICY IMPLICATIONS: NEED FOR AN OIL IMPORT FEE

A tariff on oil imports high enough to encourage aggressive exploitation of the U.S. oil resource base would eliminate these strategic concerns or postpone them to the distant future.[3] Our objective

2. "Was the U.S. Ready to Resort to Nuclear Weapons for the Persian Gulf in 1980?" *Armed Forces Journal*, September 1986, p. 92. In *The Real War*, Richard Nixon quotes former Soviet General Secretary Leonid I. Brezhnev: "It is our intention to deprive the West of its two main treasure troves: the oil fields of the Persian Gulf, and the strategic mineral resources of Central and Southern Africa."

3. A small fee applicable to some imports exists now. See February 17, 1986, statement before Senate Finance Subcommittee by J. Roger Mentz,

should be to return to the position achieved in 1979–85, when additions to reserves were equal to production. Such a fee should apply to all imports of crude oil and products. I see no reason to exempt imports from any country. If, for foreign policy reasons, it is important to help an individual oil exporting country, bilateral assistance, not exemption from the import fee, should be used for that purpose.

I have no specific recommendation on how the revenues generated by the fee should be spent. Using some of the proceeds to fund a larger program of energy research would enhance energy security now and in the future. Other alternatives, including reducing the federal deficit,[4] financing increases in the strategic petroleum reserve, or distributing the funds to the states in proportion to energy (or just oil) consumption may also merit consideration.

An import tariff would send a clear signal to oil-producing countries that the United States is going to shore up its domestic oil-producing capability and will protect this country's huge investment in its oil resources and infrastructure. That infrastructure suffered heavy losses from the oil price collapse of 1986:

—$80 billion or so in synfuels and other alternative energy systems that became uneconomic;

—the rusting and scrapping of a significant portion of the more than 3,000 rigs formerly in operation in the United States; and

—the unemployment of 50,000 highly trained professionals such as geologists and the loss of a much larger number of other jobs related to the oil industry.

Furthermore, damage from the oil price collapse is not confined to the energy industry. The U.S. economy is an integrated whole; in 1986 it became apparent that devastation in the important energy sector adversely affected GNP. That result came as a surprise. In the spring of 1986 many economists likened the reduction in oil prices to a giant tax cut that would be a boon to the U.S. economy. The

Acting Assistant Secretary (Tax Policy), Treasury, indicating these tariff rates range from five cents per barrel on certain crudes to 84 cents per barrel on certain refined products.

4. See Congressional Budget Office, *The Budgetary and Economic Effects of Oil Taxes* (GPO, 1986), which shows how the deficit would be reduced under the five proposals evaluated there.

tremendous losses incurred in the energy sector and their effect on the rest of the economy were overlooked or grossly underestimated. By mid-1986 the earlier euphoria started to wear thin. Alan Greenspan, who was chairman of the Council of Economic Advisers in the Ford administration and is now chairman of the Federal Reserve, commented in the television program "The Nightly Business Report" on June 30, 1986: "The extraordinary economic bonanza that many analysts had expected as a consequence of the sharp drop in oil prices is clearly taking its time in arriving." He further pointed out: "We are gradually beginning to understand . . . that the *sharp drop in oil prices created almost as much uncertainty and disruption as did the sharp increases* in 1973 and then again six years later [emphasis added]."

Greenspan went on to explain that the level of oil prices is a prime factor in industrial costs, but once general price levels have adjusted to new, stable oil prices, whether higher or lower, business goes on as usual and economic growth returns to its normal pace. In contrast, oil price volatility, Greenspan observed, suppresses economic activity.

On that reasoning, an oil import fee would help both producers and consumers by stabilizing the price of oil. The effect of a fee would be to put a floor under the price of crude oil. As a result, consumers would know the cost to them and producers would be in a better position to plan for the future.

Another justification for an oil import fee has been advanced by Harry Broadman and William Hogan.[5] They warn that U.S. dependence on imported oil poses a renewed threat to the country's energy and national security and call for the immediate imposition of a $10 a barrel tariff on all imports. In a subsequent study, Hogan and Bijan Mossavar-Rahmani argue that even a $5 a barrel tariff would be beneficial.[6]

The fundamental argument for a fee, according to these studies, is that the market price currently paid for imported oil by U.S.

5. Harry G. Broadman and William W. Hogan, "Oil Tariff Policy in an Uncertain Market," Discussion Paper E-86-11 (Harvard University, John F. Kennedy School of Government, November 1986).

6. William W. Hogan and Bijan Mossavar-Rahmani, "Energy Security Revisited" (Harvard University, Energy and Environmental Policy Center, 1987).

consumers does not reflect the true social cost of dependence on insecure sources of oil supply. Broadman and Hogan state that "rather than advocating protectionism for the U.S. oil industry, what we are calling for is protection for the consumers against future oil shocks." They see an import fee as an insurance policy against the risks of future disruptions.

Oil price volatility, and the uncertainty it creates, also hampers the ability of oil drillers to obtain financing for exploration. Because of this uncertainty, bankers tend to value oil at a lower price than market prospects indicate, thus reducing the amount of financing they are willing to provide. Thus at a time when the exploration and producing industry—particularly the small- to medium-sized independent operators—is in great need of capital, the value of oil is being discounted 20 percent or so because of price volatility. An import fee, by reducing that volatility, would also increase potential financing available for exploration.

In sum, a tariff on imports could become the cornerstone of a bipartisan domestic energy policy for which all can share responsibility and from which all Americans would benefit.

LUCIAN PUGLIARESI

Policy Tests for Energy Security

Contrary to the opinion of many participants in this conference, the Reagan administration does in fact believe that the United States faces a serious energy security problem. The problem stems from a specific phenomenon: the concentration of low-cost reserves in an unstable region. As a result, the United States is vulnerable to three distinct threats.

The first threat, which has happened in the past but is not now a serious problem, is the economic harm that occurs when a comparatively few exporting countries restrict output and raise the price of oil above a level that would prevail in a more competitive market. The second is the harm to U.S. economic and political interests should a major supply disruption occur. This threat becomes more serious as both the Persian Gulf contribution to the world oil market increases and the level of U.S. imports rises.

The third threat is to the sustainability of U.S. foreign policy. As both instability in the region and the Gulf's contribution to the world oil market increase, the United States will find it more difficult to sustain a collective foreign policy consensus with its allies. Some of these allies may perceive the near-term risks to their own energy security as too high or may not be able to sustain a sufficient political consensus at home to cooperate with the United States in the Gulf. This, I believe, is the point Secretary Schlesinger made here regarding the problems energy security poses for U.S. freedom of action in the foreign policy arena. This link to U.S. foreign policy makes it essential that the public, Congress, and the U.S. allies remain confident that the United States will act effectively during a major crisis in the Gulf.

TESTS FOR ENERGY POLICY PROPOSALS

Policy measures to improve energy security should be subject to several tests to determine whether they are workable. One such test is their efficiency or cost-effectiveness. A particular policy proposal may provide benefits by reducing potential GNP losses from a disruption, but will it do so enough to be worth the cost? The answer to that question may not be related to the degree of dependency on oil imports. For example, changing the level of oil import dependency may make only a modest contribution to reducing economic losses from an oil supply disruption.

Another test is whether a proposed policy package will gain the confidence of the public, Congress, and our allies. Senator McClure's earlier comment that Congress will intervene in an energy emergency provides a persuasive argument for a large strategic petroleum reserve. The SPR, for example, can assure a nervous Congress that the administration is in fact capable of responding to a crisis and thereby forestall political pressure for price and allocation controls that are likely to make matters worse. But many contributors to the conference believe we should supplement the SPR with a host of new government measures if we are to address effectively the long-term energy security threat. Presumably, the policies called for include mandatory conservation requirements, an oil import fee, a floor price for oil (a variant of the oil import fee), and subsidies or other programs to develop the alternative fuels of the future. I recommend that each policy proposal be made to pass the following tests before we give these measures serious consideration:

1. *Can the policy overcome institutional and regulatory rigidities?* How well will the proposed action hold up, considering the institutional and regulatory rigidities in the agencies that will have to carry out the proposed policy? Anyone who has sat through endless interagency meetings knows why this test is essential. Nothing short of that experience will provide a true perspective on how a policy can be distorted and undermined, to say nothing of the incalculable number of possible side effects.

2. *Is the policy sustainable over the long term?* Will the action be sustainable as circumstances change? The strategy that called for the development of synthetic fuels was directed at long-run objectives, but it could not be sustained in the face of short- and medium-term changes in market conditions and shifts in government budget priorities.

3. *How does the policy hold up under uncertainty?* Will the advantages claimed by a policy proposal be realized under conditions of uncer-

tainty? Drawdown rules for the strategic petroleum reserve are a good case in point. Too much attention is paid to determining how large the SPR should be and too little to working out the rules for acquisition and drawdown strategies. Most senior government officials prepare for a supply disruption by examining stylized scenarios— that is, a disruption of three months, six months, nine months, or twelve months. But when a disruption occurs, its duration is uncertain. The correct policy is one that addresses this uncertainty in a way that permits the policy to be effective. Here the lesson is that not only must we build the SPR, but we must have an emergency response program even when the length of a disruption is unknown.

4. *Will the policy be undermined by special interests?* A very important test of any proposed policy measure is whether the measure could, under the pressures of an emergency, be subverted by special interests. When the government placed price controls on domestic oil production and allocation controls over refinery yields and output, a whole class of special interests, such as small refiners and truckers, was created. These special interests soon became entrenched and were obstacles to more responsible policy choices.

The proposal for an import fee illustrates a similar danger. Perhaps such a fee could be kept free of special interests, but I doubt it. One would first have to extend the fee to other products as well as to crude oil to prevent it from being undermined. Then one would have to decide where to draw the line. Should the fee be extended to asphalt, methanol, and ethanol? What about products with high energy components? Then would come the pressure for exemptions— from hospitals, schools, and very likely a host of congressional interests. Unraveling of the central purpose of the fee could occur quickly.

EVALUATION OF THE REAGAN ADMINISTRATION'S ENERGY POLICY

The administration has adopted a policy that relies heavily on markets, which usually leads to effective results. However, more remains to be done. Decontrol of natural gas prices is one piece of unfinished business. Removing the windfall profit tax is another. When oil prices were escalating, the Carter administration, Congress, and other political interests believed it was inappropriate for the oil companies to receive the high profits being generated from domestic oil properties. Congress passed the windfall tax to capture some of the increased economic value of oil. Now that oil prices have undergone a dramatic decline, Congress and the administration are experiencing political pressure to bolster investment in domestic oil and gas resources.

Admittedly, the oil industry has been treated with a certain lack of symmetry. When prices were rising, Congress stepped in and removed much of the increased economic value. Now that prices have declined, it is difficult to argue that the industry should be left entirely to the workings of the market. Perhaps the best we can do now is to make a serious effort to remove the windfall tax.

Regarding the strategic petroleum reserve, more work is needed to integrate our drawdown policy into the overall energy security policy. At a minimum, we should put more effort into practicing drawdowns, and insofar as possible these should be real tests that go beyond exercising the pumps. We need to have in place a program to hold periodic auctions and actually move some of the oil into private hands. Both the government and the public must get used to the idea that the SPR is available and that it will most likely be used early in a supply disruption.

Reliance on the International Energy Agency also meets many of the tests I outlined. Specifically, the IEA builds collective responsibility for sound energy policies by encouraging the elimination of subsidies as well as providing a structure to use stocks jointly and efficiently in an emergency. However, I share many of Bill Niskanen's concerns about the IEA's sharing agreement: in the end either it will not work or it will be irrelevant.

A few comments might be useful about sustaining a constructive U.S. political relationship with nations in the Persian Gulf. The reflagging effort is not aimed simply at keeping navigation open in the Gulf. In general, our strategy must seek to maintain a position in the Gulf that will encourage friendly countries there to pursue policies that are in their long-term self-interest. In most cases those interests will match long-term U.S. energy security interests. It is true that if a regime in the region were overturned, its successor might seek to export as much, or even more oil. The transition to a stable new regime, however, could take a long time; in the interim little or no oil might be produced, which would prove costly to the United States and its allies.

In closing I would like to make a few comments about expectations. If there is one lesson to learn from our energy past, including our policies to address supply disruptions, it is that expectations are very important. We may once again face a fundamental change in expectations about the stability of the regimes as well as future production in the Gulf. A radical shift in expectations would have profound effects on the market and oil prices. We can, however, provide a stable and predictable set of expectations that the government is capable of taking responsible and effective action to address a supply emergency. If we achieve that, we will realize many of the benefits of our energy security policies.

General Discussion

Niskanen commented that it was dangerous reasoning to justify U.S. government intervention in energy markets on the grounds that OPEC intervened on the oil supply side. We should be removing impediments to the efficient functioning of markets, not adding to them because of the intervention of others.

Niskanen also noted that diversifying sources of oil for security reasons would be useful only if most oil was sold on long-term contract. If it is sold mostly on spot markets, when destinations could be changed while the oil was at sea, diversification of sources will not add to security.

Wallace argued that since governments control the production of crude oil and products, they will always play a central part in distribution. He could not understand concern about the imposition of an oil import tariff. The United States imposes tariffs on imports of such products as neckties and candy. Why not then on so strategic a commodity as oil? He sees future world competition as a struggle over natural resources. The United States should protect its natural resource base.

Howard Graeber sympathized with Wallace's concerns and asked whether our security would be endangered if the USSR gained control over Persian Gulf oil. He also asked why we could not follow the example of France and reduce our dependence on Middle East oil by meeting most of our energy requirements from nuclear power.

Niskanen said we have reason to be concerned by any development that increases the monopoly power of the oil producers. A Soviet takeover of a Middle Eastern state that would increase the amount of oil and oil reserves under their control would not serve our interest. That event, however, does not tell us whether oil production would increase or fall, which is the important distinction for energy security.

Pugliaresi thought that substantially more Soviet influence in the Gulf would be a serious foreign policy setback for the United States. The problem is real, but a tariff on oil imports would not be an effective means of addressing it.

Sharp noted that the United States spends a great deal on its military budget, the CIA, the diplomatic corps, and other programs to prevent that contingency—a Soviet takeover of Persian Gulf nations—from taking place. Furthermore, energy security is not a national matter, because oil is part of a world market. If the United States sought to insulate itself from that market, the cost would be prohibitive if it were achievable at all. It would require an oil import tariff much higher than $5 to $10 a barrel, with commensurate increases in the price of other primary energy fuels and eventually of all other prices. Energy independence as a goal advocated in the Nixon administration got nowhere politically when the cost became evident. As to France's nuclear energy option, the first point to make is that it diminishes dependence on Middle East oil for everyone, which is all to the good. On the other hand, putting so many eggs in one basket poses energy security problems if an accident occurs and all nuclear plants have to be shut down.

William Whitsit asked whether the recent action by the Agriculture Committee to mandate production of ethanol fuels despite serious environmental and economic questions is likely to typify the determination of future energy policy.

Sharp did not believe the ethanol proposal would become law. There are pork producers as well as corn growers. Production of ethanol helps one group but increases costs to the other. The fact is that ethanol is not on agriculture's agenda for energy, simply because it does not have support from all parts of the agricultural sector.

Jeffrey Jones asked what issues have to be settled to answer the question of how much energy production is needed in the United States to provide sufficient energy security.

Wallace suggested (a) developing an inventory of energy resources; (b) agreeing on the maximum percentage of imports that is acceptable, and (c) establishing incentives to ensure that domestic energy production will be sufficient to avoid exceeding the acceptable level of import dependency. Solutions may be impossible to reach, but repeated discussion of the issues is essential.

Sharp said he starts getting uncomfortable when import dependency reaches 50 percent, which is not to say our security is threatened at that point. A good, strong relationship with Canada and open relations with Venezuela would make a difference. This is one worrisome aspect about an import fee; it would harm our relations politically with countries that would be extremely important suppliers during an emergency.

Pugliaresi said we have to examine potential GNP losses associated with different levels of oil supply interruption. That is one of the natural security or economic damage risks we wish to avoid and therefore one important approach to addresssing the problem. We should try to determine how susceptible the economy is, or will be, to a major shock and then ask what measures will effectively alleviate the risk of supply interruption. Such measures include increasing the strategic petroleum reserve, improving our political and military relations with countries in the Gulf, and maintaining capability to keep the sea-lanes open. Looked at in this way, an oil import tariff does not buy much security but costs a great deal.

Fried commented that in any event the important factor is not the level of U.S. imports but the state of the world market. Higher levels of import dependency can occur with no economic disruption, or low import dependency can occur in circumstances that bring about high economic disruption costs.

Michael Koleda commented that energy security has been linked closely with oil import dependency for a long time. President Nixon wanted energy independence, that is, no imports. President Carter sought a ceiling of 8.5 million barrels a day on U.S. oil imports. Senator Bentsen and others say that imports should not exceed 50 percent of consumption. In Koleda's view, this linkage, and the emphasis on containing oil imports, is mistaken. It is generally agreed that the United States will be depending on the Middle East for an increasing share of its oil and the Middle East will increasingly dominate world oil trade. That will increase the risk of a price hike brought on by a crisis situation—military or otherwise. The strategic petroleum reserve and a military capability to intervene are the most effective instruments for such a situation.

Another risk is that OPEC in the future will become more effective in tightening supplies to raise prices gradually. The strategic petroleum reserve would do no good in such a situation, and using military measures would be unjustified. We should not rely solely on producing increasingly costly domestic oil to counter that price pressure. More effort should be placed on technologies to increase conservation and fuel switching or to produce liquid fuels from oil shale and coal. We should seek to bring down the cost of these alternative fuels and technologies, which in many cases are environmentally superior as well.

Sharp agreed on the attractions of greater flexibility and diversity in energy. Alternative transportation fuels are the key, but developing these will take a long time. We are trying to bring down the cost of photovoltaics and achieve some gains in the production of solar energy. And large funds are being spent on developing clean coal technology. None of these gains will be dramatic, but together they should make it less possible for OPEC to control the oil market. Experience has shown that OPEC wants to sell its oil and wants to avoid price actions that strongly encourage the development of alternative fuels. Companies argue that uncertainties have to be reduced if they are to make large investments in alternative fuels. Arguments then follow that the government should bear the cost of increasing national security either through subsidies, floor prices, or import fees. It is always difficult to know where to draw the line, but the danger in all these arguments is that investors are advancing a rationale that in effect asks the government to absorb risks that properly should be their responsibility.

Conference Participants

with their affiliations at the time of the conference

L. Stuart Allen
U.S. Department of State

Arthur T. Andersen
U.S. Department of Energy

J. Donald Annett
Texaco, Inc.

Mitsuhide Arakawa
Mitsui and Company (U.S.A.), Inc.

Robert L. Bamberger
Congressional Research Service

Elihu Bergman
Americans for Energy Independence

Peter D. Blair
Office of Technology Assessment

Nanette M. Blandin
Brookings Institution

Douglas R. Bohi
Federal Energy Regulatory Commission

Charles H. Broms
ARCO

Norman R. Chappell
Trans Canada Pipelines and other Canadian energy companies

Bill Clayton
U.S. News and World Report

Wendell Coote
Central Intelligence Agency

Edward Cowan
Reid, Thunberg and Company

Tom Curtis
National Governors' Association

Charles J. DiBona
American Petroleum Institute

Roger Dower
Congressional Budget Office

Andrew Drance
U.S. Department of Energy

Jerry D. Duane
U.S. Department of Energy

Joy Dunkerley
Office of Technology Assessment

Robert E. Ebel
Enserch Corporation

A. Denny Ellerman
National Coal Association

Andrew Ensor
National Security Council

Nancy Umbach Etkin
ARKLA, Inc.

Nicholas A. Fedoruk
Energy Conservation Coalition

Donna R. Fitzpatrick
U.S. Department of Energy

Christopher Flavin
Worldwatch Institute

Frederick W. Flott
Arabian American Oil Company

Tony Fountain
BP America, Inc.

Robert W. Fri
Resources for the Future

Edward R. Fried
Brookings Institution

Max Goldman
Texaco, Inc.

Joseph A. Greenwald
Attorney/Consultant

Howard Greyber
George Mason University

David E. Gushee
Congressional Research Service

John H. Guy, IV
National Petroleum Council

Robert Hahn
Council of Economic Advisers

Patricia A. Hammick
Natural Gas Supply Association

Benjamin A. Hardesty
Stonewall Gas Company

Stanley J. Heginbotham
Congressional Research Service

Bob Hershey
New York Times

Heinz Hilbrecht
European Communities' Delegation

Ann L. Hollick
U.S. Department of State

John W. Holmes
Exxon Corporation

Ethel S. Hornbeck
Petroleum Marketers' Association of
America

Hendrik S. Houthakker
Harvard University

Jeffrey A. Jones
U.S. Department of Defense

Edward Taylor Kelsch
Arabian American Oil Company

W. Calvin Kilgore
U.S. Department of Energy

James Knight
Energy consultant

Wilfred L. Kohl
Johns Hopkins University

Michael S. Koleda
Council on Alternate Fuels

Takeshi Kondo
C. Itoh & Company (America), Inc.

Lawrence J. Korb
Brookings Institution

Marvin H. Kosters
American Enterprise Institute

Elmer Lammi
United Press International

Salvatore Lazzari
Congressional Research Service

John H. Lichtblau
Petroleum Industry Research
Foundation

Bill Loveless
Inside Energy

James A. McClure
U.S. Senate

Bruce K. MacLaury
Brookings Institution

Charles M. Maguire
Consultant

Brian Mannix
American Enterprise Institute

Onnic Marashian
Platt's Oilgram News

Jan W. Mares
Executive Office of the President

Jacques R. Maroni
Ford Motor Company

William F. Martin
U.S. Department of Energy

Jessica Tuchman Mathews
World Resources Institute

Harry J. Middleton
Lyndon Baines Johnson Library

Flora H. Milans
U.S. General Accounting Office

Paul Mlotok
Salomon Brothers, Inc.

John Moore
Oil Daily

Bruce C. Netschert
National Economic Research Associates, Inc.

Marshall W. Nichols
National Petroleum Council

William A. Niskanen
Cato Institute

Trent Norris
Office of Senator Wyche Fowler

Jack H. Nunn
National Defense University

Ellen Nunnelee
U.S. Council for Energy Awareness

Robert N. Oglesby
General Motors Corporation

John R. Phillips
E. I. Du Pont de Nemours and Company

John Post
Brookings Institution

Lucian Pugliaresi
National Security Council

William B. Quandt
Brookings Institution

Rafael G. Quijano
Petroleos Mexicanos

Bill Rankin
Energy Daily

Myer Rashish
Rashish Associates, Inc.

Larry Reed
Lyndon Baines Johnson Foundation

Alfred Reifman
Congressional Research Service

Jack Riggs
House Subcommittee on Energy and Power

Henry S. Rowen
Hoover Institution

Arnold Safer
Energy Futures Group

Robert Sale
BP America, Inc.

Franklin Salisbury
League of Women Voters Education Fund

James R. Schlesinger
Center for Strategic and International Studies

Philip R. Sharp
U.S. House of Representatives

Max Sherman
Lyndon B. Johnson School of Public Affairs

Seiho Shimada
NKK America, Inc.

Margaret W. Sibley
U.S. Department of Energy

Adam E. Sieminski
Washington Analysis Corporation

S. Fred Singer
U.S. Department of Transportation

Kathleen Smith
League of Women Voters Education Fund

Austin Smythe
Senate Committee on the Budget

David W. South
Argonne National Laboratory

Charles Stalon
Federal Energy Regulatory Commission

Marshall A. Staunton
U.S. Department of Energy

Urvan R. Sternfels
National Petroleum Refiners Association

Thomas Termini
Future Resources Magazine

Stephen Tull
Alliance to Save Energy

Elena Turner
Conant Associates

Howard Useem
Senate Committee on Energy and Natural Resources

John A. Vance
Pacific Gas and Electric Company

Philip K. Verleger, Jr.
Institute for International Economics

Frank Verrastro
Pennzoil Company

Mack Wallace
Hughes and Luce

William Weingarten
U.S. Department of State

Carol Werner
Environmental Action, Inc.

William F. Whitsit
Sun Company, Inc.

Guenther Wilhelm
Exxon Corporation

Bill Wiley
Amoco Corporation

Frank Wolf
Lyndon Baines Johnson Library

James L. Wolf
Alliance to Save Energy

Mary Beth Zimmerman
National Governors' Association